release the
# HOUNDS

# release the
# HOUNDS

A guide to research for journalists and writers

CHRISTINE FOGG

ALLEN&UNWIN

First published in 2005

Allen & Unwin
83 Alexander Street
Crows Nest NSW 2065
Australia
Phone:    (61 2) 8425 0100
Fax:      (61 2) 9906 2218
Email:    info@allenandunwin.com
Web:      www.allenandunwin.com

National Library of Australia
Cataloguing-in-Publication entry:

Fogg, Christine.
Release the hounds : a guide to research for journalists
and writers.

Bibliography.

ISBN 1 74114 322 5.

1. Information services.  2. Mass media - Information
services.  3. Mass media - Research.  I. Title.

025.524

Set in 10.5/13pt Hiroshige Book by Midland Typesetters
Printed by Southwind Printers, Singapore

10  9  8  7  6  5  4  3  2  1

# CONTENTS

# FOREWORD

*Professor Bruce Grundy*

One of the best expositions I have seen of why we need journalism was written not by a journalist, but two lawyers. They had been commissioned by the government of the day to investigate the paper trail involved in a matter which had remained unresolved in one of our states for several years. It had been breaking out, like a goanna bite, in some parts of the media every few months.

When they submitted their report, they recommended that a full and open public inquiry be held into the matter. They maintained that the media had shown there had been numerous and serious breaches of the criminal law. They said:

> The investigation which we have conducted serves to underscore, once again, the importance of the media in our community, as a 'watchdog' in respect of improper conduct by governments and public authorities . . .
>
> The role of journalists in such matters is often a difficult one. Lacking any compulsive powers apart from those which exist under Freedom of Information legislation, the first problem which they frequently encounter is to secure relevant information from public

functionaries who are often extremely reluctant to extend their cooperation.

Based on such limited information as they are able to acquire, they must attempt, as best they can, to identify whether any wrong-doing has been committed, often without the benefit of legal training or qualified legal assistance, running the risk of actions for defamation if the conclusions which they reach are ultimately held to be unsustainable.

Theirs is the often difficult function of attempting to express quite complex issues in a way which is comprehensible to the readers of daily newspapers, and to the viewers of current affairs television programmes. Seldom do journalists have the luxury of publishing detailed reports, in which the evidence can be carefully weighed and examined; they must attempt to distill the issues to a degree of brevity which accords with the very limited attention span of their readers or viewers . . .

And, most of all, they face the daunting task of maintaining public interest in issues of genuine public concern, whilst the great majority of readers and viewers soon tire of one story and await eagerly the next scandal to emerge. When one considers all of the constraints under which journalists operate, one must readily acknowledge the extraordinary success achieved by a small number of journalists, in discovering many of the facts relevant to the matters which are the subject of our investigation, in identifying the possible areas of wrong-doing which those facts reveal, in compiling reports which summarise those facts with an acceptable level of accuracy, and—most importantly—in maintaining public interest and concern over issues which powerful forces in the community would have preferred to see covered-up. (Morris & Howard, 1996)

Those words are six years old. Back then, Freedom of Information (FOI) legislation was a useful tool in the journalist's kitbag. Privacy laws (which pay little or no heed to the notion of such things as public interest) were still being invented. However, all that has changed. The task has become even more difficult.

FOI is now all but a waste of time. Unless you work for a big organisation, it is just too expensive. The 'motherhood' statements, and the platitudes about accountability and transparency, and enhancing good government and democracy, are still there, but they simply priced FOI out of the range of ordinary citizens and most journalists. The user pays for everything these days, and if you can't afford to pay . . . well, too bad.

Once upon a time, the crooked or the corrupt who used the roads (paid for by the helpful public) to conduct their nefarious activities could be traced via the registration plates on their motor vehicles. Not any more—that's a privacy issue now. Privacy laws have lifted private interest well and truly over the top of public interest.

The notion of an independent public service has also all but vanished—and with it, so often, impartiality in dealing with journalists. Bureaucrats today know more than ever how their bread gets buttered—and how the mortgage gets paid. In recent times even they have been known to tell quite blatantly transparent lies to protect their political masters.

Then there is the reality that newsrooms today are leaner and meaner than ever, and the demands to achieve more and more with fewer and fewer resources are greater.

There is an upside, however: the internet. In the past, researching a story involved going through the press clippings; maybe consulting an encyclopaedia; and perhaps phoning a couple of 'usual suspects' who may have some background information. Quite often that was it.

Now there is information, quite literally, at our fingertips. Indeed, sometimes there is too much.

There is no more time available, however. This means reporters have to be able to access well-targeted, useful information—not just bulk, useless information—with a minimum of fuss and as quickly as possible.

There is plenty of useful information on the net, although some of it is well concealed. The net is also groaning with lots of useless information which should be concealed but isn't. Every Tom, Dick and Harry has a site—and who knows whether their offering is remotely of any value?

Another problem with the net is the current—erroneous—view that it is the *only* repository of information, so if something is not on the net, it doesn't exist.

That is where this book fits in. Being net-savvy is good, but being savvy all round is better. Journalism needs savvy people. Hanging out in bars is OK, but there is more to the game these days—or there should be. The task for the dedicated journalist is great. The obstacles are many. Anything that can assist is worth having, such as this book.

*Bruce Grundy*

# ACKNOWLEDGEMENTS

Many people have inspired, challenged and helped me to complete this book. My colleagues have been generous with their attention and interest, and this book would not have been begun, nor could have been finished, without their encouragement and suggestions. Journalists, as well as other researchers and writers, also very kindly read drafts and contributed advice and energy to the project.

I particularly appreciate the continuing enthusiasm for the project shown by Dr Mark Hayes. As well, educators Dr Leo Bowman, Graham Cairns, Phil Castle, Professor Bruce Grundy, Susan Hetherington, Dr Cathy Jenkins, Dr Janine Little, Dr Willa McDonald, Dr David McKnight, Roger Patching, Dr Mark Pearson, Matthew Ricketson, Dr Angela Romano, Sandra Symons, and Belinda Weaver read drafts and contributed many valuable ideas. Thanks to Elizabeth Meryment for allowing me to draw on her excellent lecture on political reporting.

Dave Barrington, Douglas Broad, Peter Carmichael, David Gormley, Helen Gormley, Thais Hardman, Tasha Milkman, Annamarie Reyes, Tom Klempfner and Dr John Wilkinson were also generous with their time and feedback.

And thanks to Steve Sharp for the title.

*Christine Fogg*

# CONTRIBUTORS

**Graham Cairns** is a lecturer in computer-assisted journalism at Queensland University of Technology, and a senior journalist with ABC NewsRadio.

**Anna Cater** is a documentary researcher and producer. Before moving into documentaries, she was head of research at the ABC Television's *Four Corners,* and before that she worked for *Background Briefing* (ABC Radio National) and as a newspaper journalist.

**Susan Hetherington** worked as a journalist with Australian Provincial Newspapers for 14 years and for Reed Regional Newspapers in England for two years. She now lectures in journalism at the Queensland University of Technology.

**Janine Little** is an academic and journalist teaching at the Queensland University of Technology and the University of Queensland. She has published widely in areas of cultural theory, race relations and gender studies.

**Siobhan McHugh** is an award-winning writer, broadcaster and oral historian. Her first book, *The Snowy: The People Behind the Power,* won the New South Wales Premier's Award for Non-fiction. She has written five books of social history and a children's fiction book. Her radio features have been shortlisted for a Walkley Award, a Eureka Science Award, the New South Wales Premier's History Awards and the United Nations Peace Prize. She co-wrote the TV documentary series *The Irish Empire*, and freelances as an oral history consultant.

**David McKnight** is a senior lecturer in journalism at the University of Technology, Sydney.

**Roger Patching** is an associate professor in journalism at Bond University, Queensland.

# INTRODUCTION

*Release the Hounds* tackles one of the biggest problems in research today—the variable quality of information resources—through concentrating on the sources of information rather than the delivery method.

After the internet broke in 1994, and as I watched students accessing information through a Web browser, I felt concerned about the difficulty they were experiencing in identifying just what they were finding in the torrent of images and words flowing across their computer screens. Although they found and used journal articles, book chapters and conference reports for their research, they were also happily finding and using information provided by unknown people on mailing lists, advertisements and primary school students' assignments.

Enthusiasts for this new technology, including myself, talked up the joys and the benefits of getting online and using email and the Web. Our enthusiasm was justified, but it had the effect of focusing attention on the delivery method, rather than the sources of information.

As well as not knowing who or what had provided the information they were using, students and researchers working online were becoming less aware of the differences between the types of people, groups and institutions which provide information.

To ring the president of your local Parents and Citizens

group and ask them to send you their newsletter, to call a contact at a union or environmental group and ask them some questions, to go to a conference to collect a paper, or to attend the AGM of a company and persuade the CEO to talk to you takes much longer than downloading documents, but doing so will help you register the differences between these sources of information. It is much harder to do this online.

This is why *Release the Hounds* concentrates on where information comes from, what information sources are, who is responsible for them and which kind of resource is likely to meet a particular need. The aim is to help users not only to put facts and data into context, but, more importantly, to use them effectively.

As well as helping students and researchers to distinguish between different sources, I want to stress that not everything is online. I wrote my previous book, *Mastering the Maze*, to introduce journalists to the wealth of resources that were available to them in libraries. Many of these riches are now online, but not all of them. There are still many unique and important resources stored in libraries and archives. To find everything relevant, a researcher may need to go out and talk to real people, to visit repositories in person and sift through files of documents.

Also, many resources are available in a multiplicity of formats and it may suit some users to access them offline. For example, many high quality directories such as the *Directory of Australian Associati*ons are not free, and most people will access them through a library. They may access the electronic version through their library's website, or it could be more convenient to consult this resource in its printed form in the reference section.

This is why I have included both online and offline material in *Release the Hounds*—happy hunting!

# MARKING THE TERRITORY

## RESEARCH FOR JOURNALISTS AND WRITERS

### David McKnight

Journalists need very specific information, about particular people and particular events. They focus on finding only the information that is relevant to the story they are working on, not on finding everything related to the issue with which their story deals.

In that way, journalism research is quite different from academic research. There is no value in getting all the information—including irrelevant data which would obscure the story. To research successfully as a journalist, you must know what your story is really about and, during the research, constantly make decisions about priorities on that basis.

Journalism research requires particular knowledge and abilities, including:

- good general knowledge;
- an interest in public affairs;
- a basic knowledge of the way the world works;
- skills in critical and analytical thinking;
- imagination, to think what an unwritten story will need;
- a streetwise approach;

- the ability to maintain a sceptical approach while researching; and
- the ability to see the connections to the political and social context surrounding an issue.

One habit which all good journalists must develop is simply to read one or two newspapers every day, and to listen to or watch current affairs programs on radio and television. Reporters find stories through using their eyes and ears, through observing and reading, and by listening to people.

Once you have an idea, you need to check out whether it can be turned into a story through asking questions such as:

- Are there interesting angles?
- Will the key people talk to you?
- Does your basic thesis stand up to scrutiny?
- Have you identified the real issues?
- Are you overlooking a better story?
- Is there a local connection?

Expect a story to change as you go along. It may turn out there is no story at all, or you may find another story or stories as your research proceeds. For instance, while looking for a good anecdote to begin your story, you could hear something from one of your sources which is so startling, new or unexpected that it would make a great intro, and this could change the direction of your whole story.

If you get that feeling that the story is dying underneath you, then cut your losses quickly. It is always tempting to keep flogging a story which does not really stand up to scrutiny.

Research for journalism is about teaching yourself so you can inform people. Reporters need to keep in touch with areas they are interested in, which means understanding intellectual ideas, as well as the broad concepts relevant to the area.

Effective research also demands a range of specialised knowledge, which can be as basic as understanding how a particular organisation is structured and how it functions. Such information makes it far easier to find and contact the people who have the information you need.

A more complex level of knowledge is needed to negotiate successfully specialised areas which have their own way of functioning and their own specialised vocabulary. For instance, science reporters need to understand how scientific credibility and the peer review process work. They need to be able to assess the credibility of research as well as understanding the science.

Research involves observation: reporters watching events or the consequences of events to record their impressions. If an event is likely to be important for your story, then make sure you are there.

Journalists also need to be able to identify and contact people—often to a tight deadline. They must be able to communicate well enough over the telephone to gain people's confidence and cooperation, and demonstrate a high degree of sensitivity to class and cultural differences to interact effectively with a wide range of people.

This kind of research involves having enough assertiveness and communication skills to approach powerful people and institutions in a confident manner. For assertiveness, you need to cultivate the 'I' language: 'I need to know . . .'; 'I need to find out the time of . . .'; 'I want the exact number of . . .'. If you are working to a tight deadline, tell people— make your problem their problem.

Research for journalism is about talking to people and reading documents, with the aim of using quotes from both types of source to build up a story. But finding the right people and documents can sometimes be hard.

Journalism values the concrete rather than the abstract,

making it vital to find specific examples which illustrate the wider topic. A journalist values first of all the person who *did* it, then the person who *saw* it and, finally, the commentator.

> For instance, for a story about poor students, finding a student who raids rubbish tins to survive will make a more vivid and memorable story than one which focuses on an expert on education funding.

The research drives the writing, so the storytelling or narrative structure is directed by what the writer finds out. If a crucial question is not asked, or a crucial statistic is not found, the whole direction of the story will be affected. If your material is thin, your story will be thin because you probably will not have time to improve it. The effect of working to deadlines means that reporters can only get what is possible by the deadline, leaving more to come tomorrow.

It is important to find out as much as possible for yourself. The best journalists are always sceptical, always think there is another side to the story and check everything themselves. It is crucial to check your sources and your state of knowledge. Good questions to ask include: 'How do you know that?' or 'Did you see that?' or 'Were you there at the time?'

Journalistic research is a continuous process. At the start, research could produce someone to interview and illuminate the background to the topic or issue. While preparing the report, discrepancies and allegations must be checked, and at the end of the process facts and figures may need to be checked and updated.

This kind of research includes a spectrum of different research methods. At one end news research uncovers stories quickly for an immediate audience, while at the other end, slow and painstaking research which can take months to complete underpins investigative stories, documentaries and books.

## A STEP-BY-STEP GUIDE TO GETTING THE NEWS

Why not just ring someone? Getting out on the street and talking to people is vital for good journalism, but your understanding is always improved if you find out as much as you can about the topic beforehand.

There are times—such as natural disasters and accidents—when you will need to go in cold and think on your feet; however, for the most part, the better prepared you are, the better your questions will be.

This is because you can ask much more incisive questions and get better quotes from your sources when you know a lot of the facts and figures before you talk to them. Being prepared also means you will be more likely to pick up omissions, inconsistencies and lies.

*Sydney Morning Herald* journalist Malcolm Brown says:

On demobilisation, I saw that journalism had something in common with soldiering: when the crunch comes and you have to react and produce results, your success depends largely on your degree of preparation. (Brown 2003)

The steps you take to locate the information you need are dictated by your destination—by what you want to find out. Taking the time at the start to clarify what you are really looking for will make the task quicker and easier in the end.

After 23 years of researching stories for ABC Radio's *Background Briefing*, Stan Correy says:

Having research skills will help to make you a good journalist but good research is not just about computers, books, magazines, having a fat contact book. All these things help you but they don't provide you with an exciting news, current affairs or documentary program.

Research is not about collecting information but about how your brain uses it. The real research skill is in making connections between what you have found, in filtering and interpreting your material to select what you need for that particular story.

It's like making cakes. People use the same ingredients but it comes out differently. Two journalists can be at the same press conference but their reports will have a different spin. (Correy, 2004)

## The story is the key

Journalism research is carried out in line with the task of writing a story. So, to research successfully, you need to know what your story is really about.

Perhaps you want to follow up the results of a new policy to supply households with water tanks. Depending on your angle, you could simply interview people who have installed tanks to find out about their experiences. Or you could focus on how much money will be saved by implementing this policy, by finding out the cost of supplying domestic water. Or you could find out what the results have been elsewhere when similar policies have been implemented.

The same general topic can produce different but equally valid stories. For instance, the topic of the Australian film industry could produce stories which say:

- The Australian film industry has had it. The glory days are over.
- Short films have revived the Australian film industry.

- The Australian film industry does particular kinds of films really well.
- Australians make great films but no-one watches them.

Your research may show that the story you are considering has already been covered to death, or that there is a far more interesting angle than the one you started out with.

**Always be prepared to dump your first idea and go after a better angle.**

To research his radio features, Stan Correy says he follows a 'crooked path':

> In the early stages imagination is important. Research is not just going in a straight line but can be following a crooked path all over the place. You should continue to question and push your material, throw the net wider and see where it leads you. (Correy, 2004)

*Sydney Morning Herald* journalist Malcolm Brown describes how he approached a current topic from a different angle to produce a fresh, new story:

> The state had been hit by the worst drought in 100 years. I knew that I had not mown my lawn for months because the grass had not grown, and it occurred to me that lawn-mower servicing shops might be in depression, along with professional lawn-mowing companies and nurseries. So I called up *Yellow Pages* online, rang some lawnmower repairers, lawn-mowing contractors and nurseries and got a great story on lawn-mowing companies laying off staff, contractors being reduced to spreading fertiliser and cleaning rubbish and nurseries making all sorts of

adaptations to patterns of demand affected by the drought. It was a fun type of story. Nobody had thought of that aspect, but it was a story there for the taking. (Brown, 2003)

## The research process

Once you have defined your story idea, you can move to thinking about how to find out what is going on, who is responsible and who will talk to you.

To help with this process, Paul, Keirstad and Shedden (2000) have supplied a list of questions to clarify what you are looking for:

- Who or what precisely is your topic?
- When and where did the relevant event take place?
- What information resource will best meet your purposes?
- Where is the biggest collection of the type of information you're looking for?
- Where might there have been coverage of the event— newspapers, trade publications, court proceedings, discussion lists?
- Who do you need to talk to?
- Who can help you to research this question?
- How much information do you really need?

For successful research, Weaver (2002) highlights the importance of developing 'information literacy', which involves knowing when you need information, how and where to get it and how to evaluate and use the information you find. Rather than a 'lucky dip' approach, she urges information-seekers to use their general knowledge about the way the world works and where information comes from to predict which person or organisation is likely to have the information they are looking for. Successful research can involve using both secondary and primary sources.

- *Secondary sources* include information which has been selected, processed and/or edited, such as articles from newsletters, newspapers, magazines and broadcast transcripts; reference books such as handbooks, almanacs and yearbooks; theses and biographies; archives, charts and maps.
- *Primary sources* include people, birth, marriage and divorce records, *Hansard* (the record of what is said in parliament), letters, diaries, survey results, menus, interviews and manuscripts.

Research can be performed at a number of different levels. While deadline pressures might mean a news story has to be covered in a ten-minute 'check the background' and call process, researching documentaries and non-fiction books usually involves a much longer process. Radio and television programs have their own special needs.

## Nosing down the news

When you are researching the news as it happens in press conferences and meetings, speeches, the courts, accidents, fires and demonstrations, you will be more efficient if you use some key tools.

- As well as checking with your contacts in organisations, look out for briefings and press releases and collect the latest news reports from news wires.
- You could also monitor lists of upcoming events, such as local government and committee meetings or scientific or industry conferences, and observe the proceedings of parliament. It could be appropriate to check out some relevant online communities for public opinion and to consult university directories to find sources and experts to interview.

## Backgrounding your stories

Backgrounding stories involves consulting resources which will explain the topic, put it into context, provide the specialised vocabulary and define some of the terms.

> As well as stories published in newspapers, archives of press releases and online communities can contain useful background information.

For big news events, collections such as the Fairfax *Sydney Morning Herald* news specials (www.smh.com.au/specials/) include links to related issues and resources and information about key players.

You can find overviews and definitions in directories, portals and reference resources such as factbooks and handbooks. To find how a significant event developed, check the chronology of the issue with a resource such as *Keesing's Record of World Events* (Longman, London).

## Specific fact research

It is often necessary for reporters and sub-editors to find the answers to questions such as:
- What is the level of rainfall in . . . region?
- How many commercial fisherpersons are there in New Zealand?
- When was . . . born?
- How much profit did . . . company make last year?

Good fact-checking resources include:
- reference resources such as factbooks, handbooks, glossaries;

- *Who's Who* for facts about prominent people;
- business websites to check their location;
- documents such as annual reports;
- statistics from government sources or research institutes;
- *Hansard* to check when a Bill was introduced;
- committee reports to get facts about a submission;
- *Government Gazettes* to find when tenders were submitted; and
- databases of legislation to check the name of an Act.

## Fleshing out features

Although research for features begins with using some backgrounding resources, this kind of research also involves foraging for more specialised information.

Using indexes and databases, specialised journals can be surveyed quickly for the latest research and developments.

Ideas on the topic nestling in web logs can be compared with those contained in newsletters published by unions, lobby groups and activist organisations.

Depending on the angle of your feature, you might need to find the relevant government agencies in order to access their documents and statistics, and to check parliamentary information, finance reports and annual reports.

It may be worthwhile to go to archives and special libraries to pick up unique resources, and to collect research findings from universities and research institutes.

Reports prepared by committees or organisations often underpin features, and representatives of groups and organisations can be important sources for information and quotes.

For example, a *Weekend Australian* feature called 'For All the Fish in the Sea', about the dangers of working as a fisherperson, included a quote from an industry group source from the East Coast Tuna Boat Owners' Association, who spoke on behalf of the fishing community. A spokesperson for Seafood Training Victoria was quoted about training difficulties. The story also referred to figures from a report on fishing safety by the UN's Food and Agriculture Organisation (Stewart, 2001).

## Investigate methodically

Investigative research involves using thorough and deep research methods to uncover hidden information, or to combine publicly available information to demonstrate the connections between people and agencies producing abuses of power, social injustice and malpractice.

As well as the above research methods, this kind of reporting often includes analysis and background, making it important to survey a wide range of material, possibly over a long period of time.

Research for investigative reports may also include collecting primary materials such as marriage, divorce statistics and child support records, as well as checking court records, bankruptcy databases and land title records.

## Crunching the numbers

Computer-assisted reporting involves taking sets of data and using spreadsheet or data-management software to record, sort and evaluate information, to analyse data using formulas such as calculating percentages and averages, and to create graphs and charts so that readers can see the significance of survey results and changes (Miller, 1998). Researchers also combine and cross-reference data sets to produce stories that demonstrate hidden connections, such as demonstrating that people of a particular race are convicted of traffic offences at a higher rate than others.

## Find the sound talent

Research for radio may include the research methods mentioned above. As well, however, radio producers need to find people who can explain their topic or their point of view on air clearly and in a way that a general audience can understand.

For radio features, atmospherics which create the program background also need to be prepared in advance. ABC Radio's Stan Correy (2004) says: 'As I'm getting the information I want, I'm also thinking about how to tell the story with sound, looking at what I can use in a radio-phonic way to illustrate the story'.

## Brief the TV team

Television researchers who retrieve and analyse information for programs such as *The 7.30 Report*, *Sunday*, *Lateline* and *Four Corners* need to know whether story ideas will work on television. As well as being on top of the full range of standard research skills in order to brief their team, they need to know how production crews work and have good teamwork skills, such as effective communication, since most television is produced by a group of people. They may also need to find locations and identify angles for telling stories visually.

A crucial research skill for television is to find and identify good talent—people who will appear credible on air. For example, preparing for political interviews on a BBC *Panorama* program about Kosovo (the 1999 NATO campaign to resolve conflict between Kosovo Albanians and the Serbian government) involved researcher Annabel Colley sourcing articles from databases and news sources to collect everything UK Prime Minister Tony Blair had said on every aspect of the war and his opinions on different people. Colley (2001) says researchers may go through twenty different sources to find two key talents, and they need to find out what that person has been saying, as well as what their exact opinion is on the strategy. The brief which Colley finally wrote consolidated all the relevant information for the program's producers.

## PROFILING A LIFE: RESEARCH FOR PROFILES, OBITUARIES AND BIOGRAPHIES

Every profile is unique, but the research can begin with you burrowing down to the spoors left by other people, before you speak to the person you are actually researching (if they are still alive and available for interview).

By looking in library catalogues, you can find out whether any books have already been written about your subject. When searching library catalogues, try a subject heading search using the person's name, followed by 'biography' or 'autobiography'—for example, 'Kofi Annan—biography'.

See 'Finding articles in indexes and databases' for help in finding articles about the subject of your story.

Is your subject likely to be mentioned in reference works such as encyclopaedias or *Who's Who*? Try the *Australian Dictionary of Biography* (Melbourne University Press) or the *Dictionary of New Zealand Biography* (www.dnzb.govt. nz/dnzb) and see 'Reference' for descriptions of other reference resources to consult.

Does your subject have their own website? A search on their name using Google, or another search engine, may turn up their site, or you could use an index such as Aussie.com Index (http://aussie.com.au) or Internic Whois (www.internic.net/whois.html) to find a website which was registered by a particular person.

If they are alive, how will you contact your subject? Finding them may be as simple as looking in the *White Pages* (www.whitepages.com.au) of the telephone book, or you could look for their business in the *Yellow Pages* (www.yellow pages.com.au). Telecom NZ (www.telecom.co.nz) has both white and yellow pages.

To find their email address, try email directories such as the Yahoo! Australia New Zealand directory of email addresses (http://au.people.yahoo.com), but it may be easier to find this out through their place of work, or by asking them directly.

If the subject's address is not in the telephone book, electoral rolls contain the addresses of people in Australia who are registered to vote. The rolls are available to the public through the offices of the Australian Electoral Commission (www.aec.gov.au). The Registrar of Electors (www.elections.org.nz/elections/conts/electors.html) holds the New Zealand rolls.

Where did they go to school and university? Newsletters or alumni records may mention their achievements.

The work your subject does or has done is a fertile field for finding information about them. If they are a registered professional, their qualifications could be recorded in data-bases such as the Law Society of New South Wales' record of lawyers (www.lawsociety.com.au), Pacific Information Resources' SearchSystems.net and the records of govern-ment bodies which register tradespeople.

Are they a creative person whose output will be recorded in galleries, museums or an archive such as ScreenSound Australia (www.screensound.gov.au)?

If your subject is involved in a business, publications such as their business website, annual reports, and newslet-ters can be checked easily. See the section on 'Digging up the business bones' for more information.

Property which they or their business owns should be recorded in land title records. See the section on 'Land Titles' below.

Donations to political parties by them or their business should be recorded in the parliamentary pecuniary interest registers.

If they have been elected to parliament, there should be records of their activities in *Hansard* and in other parliamentary records. See the section on 'Politicians, parliament' for more information.

As well as their professional activities, find out your target's recreational interests. They may belong to networks which you may be able to tap into to find people who know them.

You can locate associations through directories such as the *Directory of Australian Associations* (Information Australia, Melbourne), the *Yellow Pages* (www.yellowpages.com.au), Associations on the Net (www.ipl.org/ref/aon or www.associationcentral.com) or databases.

As an individual, are they famous or notorious enough for libraries to hold a collection of their personal papers and records? For example, the papers of governors-general are held by the National Library, and the Fryer Library at the University of Queensland holds an archive of the papers of long-time Brisbane radical Dan O'Neill.

There may be a recording of your subject talking about their work or their life. To find oral histories, see *Australia's Oral History Collections: A National Directory* (www.nla.gov.au/ohdir).

If your subject served in the armed forces, bodies such as the Australian War Memorial (www.awm.gov.au), the Office of Australian War Graves (www.dva.gov.au/commem/oawg/wargr.htm) or the Commonwealth War Graves Commission (www.cwgc.org) may hold records of their service. You could check their names in the World War II Nominal

Roll (www.ww2roll.gov.au) or try the National Library's database of official records RecordSearch (www.naa.gov.au/the_collection/family_history/armed_services.html).

Legal databases, court records and the records of legal proceedings will record whether they have sued someone or been sued.

If you are researching a person who is dead, a multitude of resources are available in archives for historical research, such as Cabinet documents, letters to local government bodies, other departmental records, immigration records, government employment records and probate on wills. See the section on archives under 'Official records' below.

## DIGGING UP THE FAMILY

Were there really convicts among your subject's ancestors? Is there any truth in the story about their great-grandmother dancing in a chorus line? Did their ancestors really come from the Ukraine?

When you are researching family history, your search may take you down many twisting paths, where you will turn up fascinating and often unexpected aspects of your subject's background.

This kind of research may begin with preparing a simple family tree before going further to prepare a detailed family history which can be produced as a book, website, CD, radio program or a movie.

### A family tree

To produce a simple family tree which shows a person's immediate ancestors, you can begin with their birth certificate, which can be obtained from the Births, Deaths and Marriages Office in each state of Australia and in New

Zealand. Links for these records are provided through Births, Deaths and Marriages Registries of Australasia (www.bdm.nsw. gov.au/bdmaus).

From there, you work back, applying for their parents' marriage certificate, their birth certificates, then their grandparents' marriage certificate, birth certificates and possibly death certificates. Next, the same process is applied to their great-grandparents, and so on.

With this information, you can create a diagram which shows the relationship between family members in different generations.

## The existing record

Now that you know the names of your subject's most immediate family, you can find out whether someone has already researched this family and published their findings and, if so, in what form.

Some *name indexes* to try are Cyndi's List of Genealogy Sites on the Internet (www.cyndislist.com), the Family-Search Internet Genealogy Service (www.familysearch.org), GeneaNet (www.geneanet.org) and Genealogy.com (www.genealogy.com).

Australian Family History and Genealogy on the Internet (www.nla.gov.au/oz/genelist.html) is a National Library of Australia portal.

If no one else seems to have gone down this particular trail, more trails are available through associations and specialised library sections.

## A guiding hand

Family history societies or genealogical associations hold resources such as archives, and run information sessions and classes.

Genealogical associations include the Society of Australian Genealogists (www.sag.org.au), the Australian Institute of Genealogical Studies (www.aigs.org.au), the Internet Family History Association of Australia (IFHAA) (www.historyaustralia.org.au) and the New Zealand Society of Genealogists (www.genealogy.org.nz).

Another way to find like-minded people and exchange information is to join an online community focused on family history, such as one of those collected in Ozlists—Genealogy (www.gu.edu.au/ozlists).

Family history sections in public and state libraries such as the Genealogy Centre at the State Library of Victoria (www.statelibrary.vic.gov.au) have resources for gathering certificates, immigration papers, parish records and photographs. Select Library Type='Local/Family history' from the Australian Libraries Gateway (www.nla.gov.au/apps/libraries) to find libraries.

Discover Family History (www.nla.gov.au/infoserv/family.html) is a guide to the National Library of Australia's resources. Genealogy/Family History (http://library.Christchurch.org.nz/Heritage/Genealogy.asp) introduces the Christchurch City Libraries' resources, while the Whakapapa portal (http://library.Christchurch.org.nz/ Guides/Whaka papa) has been provided for Maori family history researchers.

## Burrowing deeper

A full family history brings the facts vividly to life by putting the poignant or triumphant details you uncover in a historical, geographical or economic context. You can therefore record not only that your subject's great-grandmother brought up nine children alone, but she did it in a drought-stricken area during the Depression.

You may begin by interviewing family members who have documents and stories to tell about people they have known. Of course, you must expect that not all of their recollections will be true—so be prepared to check everything.

While gathering and recording their recollections, ask them about the existence of birth, death and marriage certificates, photographs, a family Bible, diaries, affiliations such as union membership, service records and diplomas.

## Looking locally

When you have some idea of where the people you are researching lived and worked, you can move to resources located there.

Although you can locate many of these resources through telephone directories, community guides or online, it can be essential for good research to go in person to facilities such as cemeteries, local libraries, museums and galleries.

Use Cemeteries of Australia (www.internment.net/aus/index.htm) to find cemeteries where you can check the records on headstones of graves, or try Which cemetery are They Buried In? (http://library.Christchurch.org.nz/guides/WhichCemetery) for some New Zealand locations.

Local libraries may have old telephone directories and collections of local resources such as personal collections. Use the Australian Libraries Gateway (www.nla.gov.au/libraries) to find libraries. The New Zealand guide, Find out about Heritage and Local History Collections, can be found through selecting <libraries> at (www.govt.nz/services).

Encyclopaedias such as *The Australian Encyclopaedia* (Australian Geographic Society, Sydney) will hold colourful details about the locality and events experienced by the person you are researching, and gazetteers such as *The Gazetteer of*

*Australia* (www.auslig.gov.au/ mapping/names/natgaz.htm) record place names from past times.

State and university libraries such as the Fryer Library at the University of Queensland (www.library.uq.edu.au/fryer/index.html) may hold manuscript collections.

Newspapers are the place to find marriage and/or birth notices. Indexes such as the *Nambour Chronicle Index 1903–1983* in state and public libraries will guide you to these notices.

The resources of local historical societies such as those listed in Local History Resources (http://localhistory.ymrl.org.au/resources.htm) can be a rich vein of clothes, photographs, tools and other memorabilia related to a particular area.

Images from galleries and the holdings of museums such as the Australian National Maritime Museum (www.anmm.gov.au) can bring the period and places you are researching to life. Australian Museums and Galleries Online (http://amol.org.au/collection) is a good place to find these resources, as is New Zealand Museums On Line (NZMOL) (www.nzmuseums.co.nz).

You may browse photographs from The National Archives through PhotoSearch (http://naa12.naa.gov.au) once registered as a guest or researcher.

Other local records which could be relevant include rate notices through local council offices, and inquest reports through archives offices, or indexes such as the *Inquest Index, Victoria: 1840–1985*.

## Official records

As well as in the area where they lived, family members' passage through life can be traced through official records in institutions and organisations.

Archives contain shipping records, passenger lists, convict records, naturalisation papers, inquest reports, probate records and wills. See the *Directory of Archives in Australia* (www.archivists.org.au/directory/asa_dir.htm), the Australian Science Archives (www.asap.unimelb.edu. au) or the Te Puna Web Directory Archives (http://web directory.nat.lib. govt.nz/dir/en/NZ/general-and-reference/ archives) to locate them.

Biographical registers or dictionaries of biography list particular kinds of people. You can track down less salubrious ancestors through the *Dictionary of Australian Bushrangers* (Hawthorn Press, Melbourne) and shining examples of achievement through *Who's Who in Australia* and the *Australian Dictionary of Biography* (Melbourne University Press).

For ex-service people, try the ex-service records in the Australian War Memorial (www.awm.gov.au), the National Library's database of official records, RecordSearch (www.naa.gov.au/the_collection/family_history/armed_servi ces.html) and the Office of Australian War Graves (www. dva.gov.au/commem/oawg/wargr.htm). The Commonwealth War Graves Commission (www.cwgc.org) holds the Debt of Honour Register, or you can check the names in the World War II Nominal Roll (www.ww2roll.gov.au).

Electoral Rolls hold the names and addresses of persons registered to vote, and are available through electoral offices in each state. See the Australian Electoral Commission (www.aec.gov.au) for locations. The New Zealand roll can be inspected at Registrar of Electors offices (www.elections. org.nz/elections/conts/electors.html), Post shops, local council offices, libraries and court offices.

Through land title information held by state government offices, you can find out about the history of the land where the subject's ancestors lived and worked. See 'Land Titles' for more information.

Organisations such as the National Trust in each state hold historical and place-related information. For example, see the New South Wales National Trust's site (www.nsw.nationaltrust.org.au/links.html) for galleries and museums.

Probate offices contain wills and other documents. State probate offices are listed below:

- ACT    Register of Probates, Law Courts of ACT
- NSW  Register of Probates, Supreme Court of NSW
- NT      Register of Probates, Law Courts
- SA      Probate Registry, Supreme Court of SA
- TAS    Probate Registry, Supreme Court of Tas
- VIC    Registrar of Probates, Law Courts
- WA     Probate Office, Public Trust Office

Statutory authorities such as the Australian Institute of Aboriginal and Torres Strait Islander Studies (AIATSIS) (www.aiatsis.gov.au) hold specialised records and databases. The AIATSIS Family History Unit assists people of Indigenous heritage to access family history resources.

## Overseas arrivals

Once you find that members of the family you are researching came to Australia from elsewhere, it is time to find the records of overseas arrivals in archives such as convict records which include lists of convicts on transports, tickets-of-leave, maps, transportation records, applications to marry and correspondence. For example, the Irish transportation records are available through the National Archives of Ireland.

Databases of overseas arrivals include *Immigration to Victoria: 1852–1879*, and Indexes such as *Immigrant Ships to New Zealand: 1835–1910* (through the National Library of Australia).

Shipping records are available through archives and public records offices such as New South Wales State Records (www.records.nsw.gov.au), or the UK Public Records Office (www.pro.gov.uk).

When you need to move your search offshore, try census records, such as the 1901 United Kingdom census (www.census.pro.gov.uk) for ancestors born in Britain, and the parish maps of the 1900 parishes in Britain. British government records can be accessed through UK Family History Online (www.familyrecords.gov.uk).

Portals such as the RootsWeb Genealogical Data Cooperative (www.rootsweb.com) include overseas information, or try GENUKI, Genealogy, United Kingdom and Ireland (www.genuki.org.uk), Web Sites for Genealogists (www.coraweb.com.au) and the World GenWeb Project (www.worldgenweb.org).

## HIDDEN JEWELS OR FOOL'S GOLD? EVALUATING YOUR INFORMATION

Good research involves being prepared to go through many sources of information, going deeper than the first available level of information, and using your judgement to select good-quality data.

Regardless of whether the source or resource you have found is online or offline, whether it is a person or a publication, a tip-off, a broadcast or a notice on a noticeboard, it is vital to be sceptical and critical about how correct, complete and credible the information is.

Generally speaking, good information comes from reputable bodies or credible people such as those within government departments, universities and research institutes, which are required to make high-quality information available to the public.

As well as coming from a reputable agency, information is more likely to be reliable when its production includes a process such as editing or peer review, where it is assessed, checked and validated.

It is also important to pay attention to where you found the data; the most valuable information may be found in specialist archives or databases where it has been selected by experts.

However, none of these conditions guarantees totally trustworthy information. Material can be edited, correct, factual and comprehensive—and still be very biased. Experts may have superb qualifications in their field; they may also have their own agendas. Messages obtained through reputable bodies can be incorrect and incomplete, and contain disinformation, misinformation and propaganda.

Elizabeth Kirk (2001) explains the difference between these three terms:

- *Disinformation* involves deliberate fabrication. Governments are one source of disinformation, which they supply to other governments, the media and the general public.
- *Misinformation* is defined by the *Oxford English Dictionary* as incorrect or erroneous information. It may not be deliberate, but just a mistake—as when urban legends are spread by misguided people who are acting sincerely.
- *Propaganda* is defined by the OED as 'the systematic propagation of information or ideas by an interested party in order to encourage a particular attitude or response'. Information which is disseminated for propaganda purposes may be correct, but the facts are selected and presented so as to influence listeners to think in a particular way—as when political parties and interest groups present the opposing point of view in a negative light to suit their own purposes.

## Interrogating your data

Good-quality and bad-quality information can come from all sources, but there are some guides you can use to assess data and decide whether or not to use it. Ask some questions:

- Who takes responsibility for the article or brochure? Who or what is responsible for this information, message or resource? What do they gain from supplying this data?
- How authoritative and objective are they? Are their qualifications relevant to this piece of information? What is their track record in supplying good information?
- Is it primary or a secondary source? A primary source is an *original document* such as an interview. A secondary source is a report on the interview. Relying on secondary sources is dangerous because you cannot afford to trust someone else's selective report. Try to check data in secondary sources against the facts within the primary document or record.
- Who was it written for—academics, scientists, industry members or the general public? If it was prepared for qualified people, it may be so difficult for untrained people to understand that you need to ask an expert to clarify it, or it may be better to find another source.
- Have the contents been edited? Resources which have been edited are usually more credible than those which have not been checked in this way. The editing presence is not always signposted: material prepared by govern-ment and educational institutions will probably have been edited, but may not say so.
- Has the information been peer-reviewed? Articles written by academics for publication in journals such as the *British Medical Journal* are sent to outside specialist reviewers for assessment before they are published.

These peer-reviewed articles are highly authoritative because they have been checked in this way. However, not all academic journals are peer-reviewed. Those which are generally say so on their imprint page.

- Why was the item created? Was the brochure or page created for advertising or marketing purposes, even though it does not look like it? Newspapers, magazines and websites may juxtapose advertising (material for which an advertiser takes responsibility) and editorial material (articles for which the publication's editor takes responsibility) so they are difficult to distinguish.
- When was the article created, written or produced? Is the information still up to date? Has something been published since which proves its claims are wrong?
- Are their conclusions backed up by strong evidence and reliable data? Is it correct? Has the factual information come from an authoritative source? To establish this, check data against that provided by other sources.
- How is it biased? What assumptions has the author made? What is their agenda?
- In the case of research findings, who funded the research? Have the conclusions been slanted to favour the organisation which funded the study?

Douglas Starr, who teaches science journalism, recommends comparing particular studies with other similar reports, and asking:
- Does the study add to or contradict the existing body of scientific opinion?
- Is it a definitive study or a work in progress?
- How does it compare to the broad consensus of scientific opinion?
- Has a report of the study been published in a peer-reviewed journal? (Starr, 2002)

## Wising up to websites

The above guidelines also apply to information found on websites, which may contain information which is accurate and reliable, and also information which is false and worthless. A press release is a press release, even if it is provided by a university.

If you wish to restrict the materials you find to those from government or educational sites, you may use search terms such as site:gov.au and site:edu.au combined with a topic such as 'biotechnology'.

Piper (2000) identifies some categories of websites that provide information which can be wrong or overly biased:

- counterfeit sites which disguise themselves as legitimate sites, such as www.gatt.org;
- parodies and spoofs which use humour to convey alternative information, such as www.onion.com;
- fictitious sites based on false countries, etc., such as those set up for educational and other purposes;
- malicious/hate sites which appear to come from an authoritative academic source, such as the Institute for Historical Review (http://ihr.org);
- product sites which do not make it clear that their primary purpose is marketing. These may include links to 'information for research projects' which appear to be reliable but which include a restricted set of data favourable to the product;
- science and health websites with misinformation such as simple cures for cancer; and
- fraudulent business sites which make false claims about business achievements to influence investors and share prices.

It is important to know which individual, group or organisation is responsible for the website. If you are unsure, a Whois search will show you who owns the domain name, using the Asia Pacific Network Information Centre (www.apnic.net), www.checkdomain.com or Network Solutions (www.internic.net).

Ultimately, you must ask yourself for what purpose was the site set up—information or marketing? Does the site really cover the areas it says it does? A commercial site may be set up to look like a research site. When was the content created or updated? Are all the documents on the site dated?

## Nailing down databases

Although the contents of databases may have been compiled and selected by experts, there can still be problems which may limit their usefulness. A database is a collection of information which is structured in some way so it can be retrieved. Databases can contain published stories, reports, studies, public records, and so on.

Some of the most widely used databases are those which offer access to the contents of newspapers and periodicals. A common problem of using databases of news stories uncritically is that mistakes are perpetuated, as stories may contain inconsistencies and inaccurate statements.

Not all the stories in a newspaper will make it into databases of that publication's contents. Stories written by freelancers may not be included, or those which originated in wire services, or the publication may provide a different version of a story from the one actually printed.

Some web-based databases are high in quality, but others have many of the same problems that websites face. They may have been created by people who are not experts in their area and whose motivation is suspect. Their contents may not be able to be retrieved effectively, and they may not be updated frequently enough to be reliable.

## Querying the figures

Reporting quantitative data produced through surveys without asking where the figures came from can lead to some very misleading reports about the subject surveyed. For example, surveys which purport to show that 75 per cent of the people sampled say they would vote for a particular political candidate are only reliable if the data were compiled using a statistically valid method.

Goot (2002) suggests a range of questions to ask to avoid uncritically accepting the results of polls which may not have been conducted using valid methods.

He points out that the method of sampling and the sample size are crucial indicators of a survey's reliability. It is important to know whether the respondents were selected from a known population with a more or less equal chance of being selected, or whether they were self-selected.

Market research organisations may put together 'focus groups' (who express their opinion through discussion) by selecting people via methods other than the random selection process, which ensures a statistically valid result. Although researchers often report the findings from group studies as if they could be generalised, focus groups almost never allow a statistically valid generalisation. The selection methods are rarely random. Even if they were random, the same information is rarely collected from each member of the group. And, even where both these conditions are met, the number of participants is usually so small, and the sampling error so large as a consequence, that it is impossible to say very much with any degree of confidence. Properly used, focus groups have other, much more useful functions, however.

Goot also suggests that reports of polls should include the exact wording of the question asked, together with background information such as the response options which respondents were given. For instance, when the response options are 'forced choice', respondents can only respond to a proposition such as 'Most people are worried about job security' by choosing from a limited number of options such as 'Agree', 'Disagree' or 'Unsure'. When the response options are 'open choice', the respondents feel free to express their true opinion.

It is also advisable to include the date of the survey and note whether any questions asked of respondents before the survey proper began could have influenced the answers they gave to the survey questions.

Respondents may also be influenced by the survey itself—especially by questions that precede the question in which a reporter is interested. However, Goot also points out that polls rarely explain what the preceding questions were.

So, the layers of data through which you sniff in search of reliable information is littered with appealing nuggets that may or may not turn out to have a solid core that can stand up to a good chewing. And the real gold may be buried so deep that it will take a lot of digging to bring it to the surface.

But instead of gulping them straight down, the process of turning the nuggets over, gnawing at them and tossing them around to see what they are made of will help you to distinguish the gold from the dross.

# 2

# PICKING UP THE SCENT

## FRIENDS AND FOES

Talking to human sources is a crucial research tool. Journalist Pilita Clark (2003) says:

> For me, the most successful research tool by far has been the face-to-face interview. Mining databases can sometimes yield important stories and so can an FOI application and a careful search of annual reports and government gazettes. But when I think about the journalists whose stories I have admired most over the years, they are almost always people who have taken the time to sit down and talk with other people.

If you will be researching in a particular area for any length of time, the research process includes getting on friendly terms with people who operate in this arena—preferably well before you need to ask them for information.

### Contacts

You can introduce yourself to potential contacts at public meetings and events, press conferences, displays, forums, conferences, launches, the meetings of organisations and in online communities. Public relations people will put you on mailing lists to receive newsletters and annual reports, and you can join online mailing lists for the area yourself.

Key contacts could include practitioners, members of industry and government bodies and the office-bearers of associations. Try to establish a friendly but professional relationship with these people.

As an example, if you are working in the education area, you might get to know teachers and head teachers from public and private schools, the office-bearers of the teachers' unions, P&C representatives, the staff of the minister and opposition spokesperson for education and the leading public servants in the Education Department.

Through keeping in touch like this, you can stay up to date with current news and events, how issues are developing and changing, and who is in and out. It is useful to know enough to be able to anticipate what may happen, rather than having to wait for it to happen.

## On and off the record

The ethical requirements of talking to sources include specifying who you are and explaining that you are looking for information to prepare a story for publication or broadcast, agreeing to honour any restrictions which the person speaking to you imposes on your use of their information, such as specifying that they are speaking 'off the record'.

'On the record' means that you can use all of the information you have been given and attribute it to the person who gave it to you. Terms such as 'off the record' and 'background' mean different things to different people so, rather than relying on these terms, it is preferable to ask your subject what they want to see in print, and be prepared to negotiate this with them.

## Following the crooked path

You may need to talk to many people before finding the sources you actually need. ABC Radio's Stan Correy (2004) illustrates how the process often works:

> It often happens that one person leads to another and to another. The first person you ring won't be the person you want to interview.
>
> For example, for one program I was looking for information about government involvement in diamond mines. I was reading a history studies journal and I found an article written by a historian about the involvement of the De Beers company in the Argyle diamond mine in Australia in the 1970s.
>
> The academic who wrote this article directed me to another academic who was an expert in African studies, who gave me another name overseas for an expert in diamond mines in Sierra Leone. This led to another academic based in the USA who was researching Sierra Leone, and from there to the mercenary company Executive Outcomes, which was what my program *The Diamond Mercenaries of Africa* was about.

In the course of putting stories together, participants, official spokespeople, commentators, experts and sources will not only give you information, but also the quotes you need for a report that works.

## Participants

Journalist and journalism educator David McKnight (1999) says a vivid, relevant quote can be more valuable than a dull comment by a dry expert. So, for a story about women in sport, the most valuable parts of the story will focus on a sportswoman and perhaps her coach rather than academics or sports commentators. This is because interviews with participants give us a more engaging personal perspective and greater insight than those with experts who can quote statistics but who are one step removed from the action.

## Official spokespeople

Official spokespeople could be public relations staff or a senior member of staff. If they are publicists for politicians, government departments or companies, they will probably be very experienced in dealing with the media. See the section on 'Public Relations, press releases' for more information. Spokespeople for activist organisations are usually very adept at being interviewed. However, they may be neophytes who need to be treated carefully, depending on where they stand on the scale between paranoia and recklessness.

ProfNet (www.profnet.com) is an international cooperative of public information officers. Some are attached to universities, while some are located within government departments or non-profit organisations.

## Commentators and experts

Commentators have more distance from the issue but still have an informed opinion on it. These experts have skills, training, experience or education that means they can comment on a topic with authority and credibility.

For example, an expert could be a scientist who has done a study on the topic or a community campaigner who is for or against the issue. As well as formal qualifications such as PhDs, their credibility could come from experience, such as spending years rehabilitating injured bats, winning scrabble competitions or running a business.

They may be the only people who understand a new process or a specialised topic such as long-range weather forecasting, and who can explain it in a way that will mean the general public can understand its significance.

Experts with formal qualifications can be found through their employers, such as universities and research institutions. Use the university directories, such as those provided by the University of Melbourne (www.unimelb.edu.au/contact) to find their academics.

You can find lawyers through community legal centres and specialist lawyers through the Law Societies in each state. Australia Policy Online (www.apo.org.au) contains links to experts at research centres.

People whose expertise arises from experience rather than from formal qualifications can be tracked down through their affiliations, such as the associations listed in the *Directory of Australian Associations* (Information Australia, Melbourne), which is available in public and university libraries.

Locate other experts in telephone directories, at Australian Directories (www.mrp.net/phone.html) which contains contact information for large organisations, and the Expertise section of the OzGuide (http://journoz.com/expert.html).

The records of booksellers such as Amazon (www.amazon.com), Booksmith (www.booksmith.com) and library catalogues show who has written a book on the topic, or use contacts lists such as Sources and Experts (http://metalab.unc.edu/slanews/internet/experts.html), which also includes a clearinghouse for experts.

The annual reports of companies and departments often include lists of consultants they have engaged, or check the lists of submissions in the final reports of inquiries. Through using word of mouth—your personal network—you can also turn up experts who are recommended by someone known to you.

## Sources

People who are both friends and foes will give you crucial facts, quotes and intelligence. To find sources for in-depth stories, ask yourself who will know how things really work, and who knows them.

Good sources are often people who are involved with the situation, but in a different way from the key players. Customers, cooks, clients or competitors could all be sources; information can come from movers and shakers, or from secretaries and waiters.

## Tip-offs

Your research might begin with a tip-off. People will bring stories to you if you are known for having an interest in a particular area, giving you information or problems they would like addressed.

It is important to be wary about their reasons for approaching you, and to evaluate them with the same scepticism you would apply to the sources of all information. However, try to be tactful. You can ask them to substantiate their claims, but avoid talking down to your sources. They feed you, and you need a reputation for being approachable to get tipoffs.

## Whistleblowers

Whistleblowers are people inside organisations who choose to make information about that organisation publicly known, often by passing it to a journalist. To protect them from repercussions, they usually wish to keep their identity secret, and they may make initial contact by sending an email from a free email account. A prospective whistleblower and a journalist may need to exchange a number of emails and phone calls before they can decide whether to trust each other enough to work together.

## Leaks

If data are leaked to you, you need to apply even more scepticism, since you may not know who was responsible for a document arriving on your desk.

Information may be placed online by potential sources, perhaps via their own website. Websites put up by individuals and groups may contain valuable information, but such material needs to be checked out thoroughly.

A single person might know something valuable, but they usually do not know the whole story; so rather than accepting one person's account, ask for documentation, make your own inquiries and get the different perspective offered by other sources or groups before using such information.

## EXERCISE

Find a recent story dealing with one of these topics: agriculture, business, education, the environment, health, politics or technology.

Find and interview four people who could be sources for a follow-up story about this topic:
- One of them should be a source who has an agenda, such as a member of a lobby group.
- One of them should be a participant or a witness to actual events or be personally linked to an actual event.

- One of them should be an official spokesperson for the topic.
- One of them should be a commentator or an expert on the topic.

(Adapted from an exercise devised by Dr David McKnight, University of Technology, Sydney, 1999.)

## SIFTING DOCUMENTARY SOURCES

### Anna Cater

There are two types of research for TV journalism and documentaries:
- researching the facts and opinions of a story; and
- finding good 'human interest' characters to illustrate the story.

However, to find good characters you still need to know your facts.

I once conducted research into the Stolen Generation for a documentary for the ABC and the BBC, long before there was an inquiry and the ensuing media attention. Our particular focus was into the churches' historical role. Obviously, we could not cover the thousands of indigenous peoples' and missionaries' stories (we were only looking for about five case studies), so we had first to do some very broad research throughout Australia and then, armed with this information, we could begin to make informed decisions about the people we wanted to feature to best illustrate the major themes of the film. Without knowing all the facts, we would not have been able to justify the selection of the five characters and feel confident that we were accurately portraying what had happened, and why.

I often describe research as being like an inverted pyramid. You start with finding out everything about the story and then narrow it down to a very small focus. This apex becomes a way to tell the larger story. With most research for TV journalism and documentaries, only about one per cent of the information you gather ends up in the final story or film.

What makes a good character? The audience needs to emphathise with them. This doesn't mean the audience has to like them or the character has to succeed, but the audience has to *care* about what happens to them. Unfortunately, a person's delivery is almost as important as the message they have to deliver. Characters need to have passion and to speak in an engaging way. The more they wear their hearts (and convictions) on their sleeves, the better. I always think that if I'm bored listening to a person in the research stage, then the audience is probably going to feel the same way in the finished film.

You can never be 100 per cent certain in your research that the character you choose is going to deliver when they are filmed. Mostly, your judgement will be sound, but occasionally boring people will come alive in front of the camera, and vice versa.

My specific tips for research are:

- Use the internet as a starting base for your research and get to know what's credible on it. The internet is also helpful for finding people's email addresses and telephone numbers, especially scientists and academics.
- Read everything available on your research topic. Your local library is a convenient source of books to take home and use for reference.

- Get all the newspaper clippings. I subscribe to both the Fairfax and News Ltd archive libraries on the internet, and know my way around most major libraries. Often, librarians will have a particular topic of interest so they can also be helpful.
- Read at least one major metropolitan newspaper each day so you are up to date with what is happening.
- Keep any clippings which interest you, or you think might come in useful one day.

Talk to everyone involved in the topic—one thing leads to another. At the very least you will get a better feel for the topic and who's who. There comes a time when you know you are on top of the topic, that no one is going to add much that is new. If you are not on top of the topic, admit to people that you are in the early days of research. Don't pretend, it shows. This is all part of building trust. Be careful what you say to people as your knowledge becomes valuable and can be a trading device for further information. Also, you may want to keep an element of surprise for the filmed interview. A person's reaction can be very insightful, so feel your way very carefully in research interviews.

By talking to everyone, hopefully you will strike the key person. They know everything and everyone and can guide you in sorting out what is important and what is merely distracting. This confidant may not give you any new information, but they can be a good barometer as you go deeper into your research and need to check information and peoples' bona fides with an insider.

Cultivate your contacts and keep returning to them. Throughout your career you will keep coming back to people, not just for the current story. There are people in communities who are really good at networking and are prepared to give you lots of assistance, especially in finding suitable characters. Your friends might even be able to help with characters—don't discount anyone.

It is vital to establish trust and, always, to be polite. Never be aggressive. Be aware that as a researcher, you are always 'taking' from people, and it's good to be able to 'give' something back (perhaps a copy of a report or suggestions on how to find the right assistance for their particular problem—if they have one). Also, be aware that when a person gives you their story, you are taking on a responsibility. It's a reciprocal arrangement, not a one-way street.

As often as possible, meet people face to face. They can then work out if they want to cooperate with you. Talking to them over the phone isn't an ideal way to establish a good rapport. People need to be able to look you in the eye to gauge whether or not they can trust you. Also, people tend to respond well to being listened to, and being the sole focus of someone's attention. At these preliminary meetings, I often don't take notes, as it puts people on guard if you are writing down what they are saying. It also means that you can't look at them directly, as your head is down, writing. In these instances, I just remember as much as I can and, as soon as I walk out the door, I write down what's just been said.

Being honest and acting with integrity is vital not just for the current project but for future ones. Ask direct questions, and be open about your motives and what you are trying to achieve. It's important for you to be clear in your own mind as to the content and direction of your story. These days, it takes a lot of convincing for subjects to talk to you, as there is a lot of mistrust of the media, so any slyness or uncertainty on your part will make others wary. People need to be reassured about opening up to you, and they want to know early on how their story is going to be used.

In investigative research, it's always good to find someone in the story who is disillusioned, who has been sacked, or who is an outsider in some way. This person will be more likely to tell you what's really going on. They have less to protect and want to air their grievances, even if only in private.

Information that is given off the record will help you find out what's happening behind the scenes and you can then use this information to interview people who are prepared to go on the record. Off-the-record information can also help you fill in the jigsaw puzzle.

For TV journalism and documentaries, find out what people are doing, as events in their lives can be good filming opportunities. People often think events in their lives are not that interesting or significant, so they don't tell you what's coming up unless you ask them and pin them down.

I do all my research in A4 notebooks and I have kept these for the past 15 years. This means I can easily go back to a story and find contacts and phone numbers for other projects.

## INTERVIEWING

### Roger Patching

As a simple definition, a journalistic interview should aim at getting from the person being interviewed, *in their own words*, facts or opinions on a particular subject, or reasons for a particular course of action. In the reporting of news, the readers/listeners/viewers should be able to make up their own minds on the validity of what is being presented to them, preferably by reading or hearing the person's own words.

Anyone that grants you an interview is doing you a favour; journalists have no right to demand that someone talk to them and even the most publicity-hungry public figure has the right to refuse. Often the person approached is only agreeing to be interviewed to get publicity for their opinion (or latest book, movie or CD), so be aware of the barrow they are pushing.

Interviews can be done in several ways: face to face, over the phone, by email, or by SMS message. Seasoned journalists maintain nothing beats a face-to-face interview because you can see the reaction to your questions. Phone interviews are popular with print and radio journalists seeking quick answers. Email or SMS interviews are only for the lazy, those who lack the confidence to approach and talk to people, or those who have plenty of time to wait for a reply.

Here, in summary, are some general guidelines:

- Background yourself as fully as you can on the topic before you start looking for people to interview.
- Make sure that you speak to the most appropriate people. Take the time to find the best people to interview on the particular topic.
- If you are discussing a controversial issue, present all sides. Most issues are multi-faceted.
- Prepare some questions and a general thrust for the interview(s).
- *Listen* to what you are being told. Don't be so keen to ask the questions that you have prepared that you

do not listen to what you are being told. Listen so that you can ask the follow-up question that will lead the person to elaborate further on an interesting (and new) aspect of the story.

- Never end an interview with a question unasked. Find out as much as you possibly can before you start writing. If you don't ask the questions, your audience may never know the answers. And you'll look foolish if there's a better story there and the opposition gets it.

There are three distinct types of interviews: informational, emotional and interpretive or background interview.

## The informational interview

As the name implies, this type aims at providing information, such as a simple news interview. An event has taken place—an accident, an opening of a building or a conference—and you talk to a person or persons about what they saw or heard or said. They have the information and you ask as many questions as it takes to gather sufficient facts to write your story. Depending on the questions you ask, the descriptive power of your interviewee and your writing ability, the audience gets a word picture of the event or story.

An example could be a representative of an organisation—government or private—announcing a decision that has been made, and explaining how it will be implemented. Decision-makers such as politicians and public figures at all levels are interviewed often. In most centres, a relatively small group of people make most of the news. They're called 'sources of information' and, from the journalists' point of view, they need to be nurtured because they can provide a continuous stream of news.

Another example is the eyewitness to an event, like a serious accident. You take down their account of what happened, and that becomes the basis of your description of the accident.

In this type of interview, you are only seeking facts. While you may well think you know the answers to the questions before you ask them from your background knowledge of the event, you still need verification. In these cases, the person you are talking to is an expert in the field—otherwise you would not have approached them—and while you may know some of the details, you want their version. You are relying on them to fill you in on the details.

## The emotional interview

The next type is the emotional interview. This is the type most criticised by the public. At one level, it is where someone is asked how they feel about losing a member of their family in a plane crash or a road accident. People are interested in other people's feelings at times of stress. It could be a personal tragedy, but equally it could be a time of supreme achievement, such as the national cricket team winning the World Cup or someone winning Olympic gold.

But there are other emotionally charged occasions: unionists bitter with the bosses over a long-running strike; or mothers linking arms across the road in front of the local primary school because a child has been hit by a car. Emotions are running high, and capturing that emotion is your job. It is the strength of feeling that you are trying to capture, and your questions need to be framed thoughtfully.

Then there's the person who has been thrust into the news at a time of personal tragedy and knows little about how to handle the media attention. Such a situation calls for the utmost tact, sensitivity and compassion.

## The interpretive or backgrounding interview

This is where the basic news story is already known, and you are seeking to explain the background or put the story into context. You go to the experts not for the simple facts, but for the interpretation, for answers to the 'why' or the 'how' of the story. If we take one of the examples above, you might want to interview the relevant Cabinet minister about a government decision. Why was it made? What will it mean? What were the political considerations in the decision? When will it be implemented? Where?

Then you talk to the opposition spokesperson and to those affected by the decision to get their side of the story. There's an old definition of this type of story (called 'current affairs' on radio and television) which says that, while the news reporter is at the scene of the fire, the current affairs reporter is back at the fire station interviewing the fire chief.

While preparation is important for every assignment, it is even more important for an interpretive or background interview. You start in your organisation's library. If you are a specialist reporter—government rounds, police rounds, local government, defence, the environment, sport—you will probably have kept your own background files on stories and issues. But start at your organisation's library and then branch out to the myriad of resources detailed in this book.

You need to find out all you can about your story. How else will you know if what you are being told is 'news'?

Maybe someone famous is coming to town. What can you find out about him or her? Who could tell you something about the person, what they're doing here, what they hope to achieve?

No matter who the interviewee is, there are people who can give you valuable background information about the person or their job that will help you understand more about what they are likely to want to talk about.

## Preparing for interviews

The more time you spend on preparation, the better your interview will be. The reverse is equally true. The worst interviews—and, usually, the worst stories—result from being thrown into an interview situation without having had time to research. It should *not* happen, but it does—all too often. That's where reading the papers and keeping abreast of radio or TV news and current affairs programs will help. Journalists need to know something about everything—enough to start researching or, at worst, to start an interview.

Take time to work out some of the questions you would like to ask the person or persons being interviewed for the story. Never go to an interview without at least a starting list of questions.

Use the 'five W's' of news story writing—the who, what, where, why, when—as well as the how. They are equally important. The best questions start with those five W's and the H. In many stories, it is the *why* and *how* that are the most important.

Write your questions on a piece of paper. What do you really want to get out of the interview? What are the most important pieces of information you need to discover? From your research, what sort of angle can you take? You need to have some idea of an angle for the story before you start, even if you find that your preconception of the story doesn't work out as expected.

## Conducting the interview

For a news story, you are interested in quick interviews—a few minutes at the most, as often as not over the telephone, because you can't afford the time to visit the person or persons involved.

But whether it is a news interview, or a longer one for a feature, you need to be courteous, and look and sound interested in what the person is telling you. If they see or hear that you are interested, your interviewees are more likely to respond to your interest with informative answers.

Don't be afraid to ask someone to elaborate or explain something if you don't understand, particularly if they talk in jargon. All industries, enterprises and government agencies have their own language and acronyms—if you don't understand, just say so.

Don't leave the interview with a question mark in your mind about anything you asked, or anything your interviewee said. Always get a telephone number so you can call back in case you need to check something later. Give the person your business card. Get theirs in return.

As a general rule, don't ask questions such as:

- 'Do you agree that...?' You'll probably get a 'yes' or a 'no', and little else;
- double-barrelled questions—two questions in one; it can be confusing; and
- 'either/or' questions, because they restrict the interviewee's choice.

Don't be afraid to play 'the devil's advocate'. That's where you put a position to the person you are interviewing, and expect them to present the counter-arguments: 'What's your reaction to the criticism that . . . ?'

## News conferences

Often, you will be part of a news conference. Someone calls in the media to announce something, release a report or introduce someone famous.

Again, prepare as best you can before the event. Think of a few questions. Make sure you ask *your* questions and don't be intimidated by others' questions. Any answer to a question at an open media conference is available for anyone to use. If you think you have a line of questioning that no one else has thought of, then approach the person after the interview to spend a few moments in private, so you don't give the other reporters your story idea.

Preparation also includes making sure your equipment is working properly, and that you have an additional cassette or mini-disc available. It's too late if something goes wrong in the middle of an interview. You look stupid if you have to excuse yourself to head for an electrical store to buy a cassette, and even sillier if the batteries run out or your mike doesn't work.

## The feature interview

Doing an interview for a feature or colour piece, or a piece backgrounding a person or event, is quite different to the purely informational, or emotional, interview.

Whereas a simple news interview might take only a few minutes, an in-depth interview for a feature will require a much longer interview, especially of the central character of the piece. It may be a personality piece, for example, a background report about a sporting personality, the club they play for, their coach, or an international entertainer appearing locally.

Famous people, or those who have done many interviews in the past, are relatively easy to deal with. They know what you want, and for those who want publicity— a popstar promoting a forthcoming tour or current CD, an author whose book has just been released, or an actor publicising their latest film or TV series—it is often a matter of trying to keep them on the track of what you want them to talk about, rather than letting them spread the message they want to get across at every whistle-stop on their tour.

Politicians and other leading public figures are much the same. They arrive with a set message they want to communicate, and if you want a successful, or different, feature on them, it is up to you to keep them going along your train of thought, and not be derailed by what they want to push. By all means let them have their say. Don't interrupt, but if what they are saying is not relevant to what you are after, quickly get them back on track.

The hardest feature-style interviews are those with people who have become, virtually overnight, a celebrity, or with someone who, for some reason or other, does not trust the media.

First you have to get their confidence. Always do feature interviews in person.

An example is someone local who wins an international competition—say in boxing—so your newspaper decides to profile him or her. Let's assume that they are not used to dealing with the media, and you organise to meet them, possibly at their home or somewhere mutually convenient, to have a chat. Always ask where they would like to do the interview; they'll feel much more comfortable in familiar surroundings than sitting across the desk from you in the office or in an intimidating radio or television studio.

Get as much background as you can on the person before you meet them: it's a form of flattery that usually works. They will know you are serious because clearly you have tried to find out as much as you can about them.

Ask open-ended questions, such as, 'How did you get involved in boxing?' Try to show, by the way you ask the questions and your comments about their answers, that you know something about them and their sport.

Ask about their training schedule, who was the biggest influence on their career, why they decided to take up the sport, who they admire, whether they're finding fame difficult to handle, their goals now, how they relax away from competition, and so on.

Try to get under the façade of the new champion. What are they really like? What can you tell your audience about this seemingly super-human athlete, that makes them special, or just like one of us? You rarely know what the answers will be, but any of those lines of questioning could lead to some colourful anecdote(s) for your feature, and make the champion a personality as well as a winner. You're looking for something that hasn't already been plastered across the media.

The same sort of questioning could be used for an entertainer, but it is usually harder to get under the veneer of someone who is interviewed day in, day out. They tend to have glib answers for everything.

I once attended a news conference with the Beatles in Adelaide in the early 1960s. They enjoyed making fools of interviewers. 'How did you find America?' one reporter asked, knowing they'd just had a very successful tour there. 'Turn left at Greenland,' the late John Lennon said. 'What do you think of Red China?' someone asked. 'It looks great on a white tablecloth,' Paul McCartney replied.

Funny? Yes, but obviously rehearsed so that they didn't have to give political answers.

What about an interview with a representative of a company that is about to enter the international market, or has done something special but is wary of the media? Maybe a reporter has misquoted them in the past, and they have been rapped over the knuckles by their superiors. If you think the person doesn't like the media for some reason, ask them to talk about it. Get it out in the open and discuss it. Try to gain their confidence. Show that you care about getting it right, and are giving them the opportunity to set the record straight.

What types of questions should you ask? Find out about the local impact of the move, how many jobs will be created, the history of the company, details of the expansion plans, what they need to do to crack the international market, where the opposition will come from, and what makes the interviewee think their product is so good—in short, anything you can think of to keep the person talking.

A lot of interviewing involves thinking on your feet, considering where the previous comment might lead. What does the person really mean? Ask questions aimed at making them justify their position or comment, but don't be argumentative.

Don't overstay your welcome—but don't leave without asking the important final question: 'Is there anything I haven't asked that you'd like to add?'

For more information about interviewing, see McGregor and Sedorkin (2002).

## WORKING CONTACTS: FINDING AND KEEPING RELIABLE SOURCES

### Janine Little

Ask any productive reporter how they manage to come up with so many good yarns, day in, day out, and they'll probably point straight to their contact book—the thing we'd grab first if a fire broke out in the newsroom. We would grab it before the notebook, since an interview can always be redone and research always retrieved, but phone numbers and names gathered—often through years of work, in many different places—are not so easy to replace.

This points to two reasons for the inclusion of this section in *Release the Hounds*. First, inexperienced journalists will discover quickly that the journalist with a healthy contact book might point to it, but will never let you look inside. Journalists should never share their contacts with colleagues. (There is a significant difference between a contact and a media liaison/public relations person, one which will hopefully speak for itself by the conclusion of this section.)

Second, the ability to find and maintain contacts is the key to activating journalism's interventions into institutions and ideologies of power, through its essentially social role.

Journalism schools stress detachment from sources as an assertion of core news values of fairness, balance and objectivity. However, there is a finer distinction to be made between detachment, and investment in your reputation as a reporter who can be trusted and relied upon to look after good contacts. The current nature of journalism education, within the broader cultural effects of trends in information production and consumption, means that inexperienced reporters may not recognise the importance to the bigger picture of developing independent sources of information. Working contacts, then, is as much about journalism's social role as about the importance of practising journalism with what Brooke Kroeger (n.d.) refers to as 'a scholar's intent'. See also Bromley (2002), which emphasises the importance of graduating journalists being 'comfortable with methodologies and theories, reflective practice and action research'.

Before electronic newsrooms and overarching corporate structures, journalists spent a lot more time outside the office. There was a good reason for this: being around the places where people significant to your round congregated increased your chances of finding stories. Often these contacts felt a lot more comfortable talking to a particular reporter after seeing them in an informal environment, where some level of social rapport was achieved.

The pub, for example, was a representation of journalism's social/professional admixture. It provided space outside the confines of various structures of authority for reporters to blow off steam, but also to make themselves known to the people behind the structures, and to put faces to names. In regional towns, where the majority of today's senior roundspeople cut their reporting teeth, this was especially so.

The regional newspaper reporter remains the epitome of community journalism, with the reporter's profile within that community often measured alongside their social relationships. Since reporting at a metro level is no less a social job, and its social nature has not diminished with the growth of the internet, similar principles apply to building and working contacts. You have to be seen to be out and about, rather than becoming a 'telephone jockey' or, these days, an email processor.

Getting out and about should never stop at merely attending media events hosted by public relations officers and other corporate concerns. These are useful for networking and meeting people 'of note', but news reporting is also about offering an ear to the relatively powerless, or those not prone to turning up at lavish lunches at five-star hotels or Parliament House.

Union officials, truckdrivers, lower-level public servants, beat police, backbenchers, lobbyists and people who know people who work with other people are all potential gold veins of quality information. Keeping your ears and eyes open and being approachable but not too gullible, are the keys to finding such sources.

Once you've started to get to know people, how do you establish them as regular contacts? First and foremost, you should *never* ask them if they want to be your contact. A recent Morgan Gallup Poll showed newspaper journalists are still rated below used car salesmen, real estate agents and even pedophiles on the public opinion scale. This, and people's natural tendency for self-preservation, means it's going to take a while for you to earn their trust. It's also going to take even longer to earn the confidence of people who initially may dismiss you as inexperienced, naïve, or just not a good bet for understanding what they tell you or, crucially, doing something with what they tell you. To go straight in and ask someone to be your contact does little more than expose your *lack* of contacts.

If you've got no (or few) runs on the board in terms of front news page bylines, subjects may not have heard of you or read your copy. In these circumstances, the best way to begin is by being laid back: talk about the cricket, *then* about what you've seen happening in their particular area of occupation. This shows that you're not only interested in them as a person, but also that you're up with the latest events and have actually read what's been in the news. Then have another conversation about cricket, or surfing, or where they went on holidays. Like any social relationship, it works on a quid pro quo basis: you tell them a bit about yourself, they feel they can tell you something, and so on.

The golden rule here is NEVER repeat anything you hear outside these conversations—not even to your colleagues. If you do, it will get back to the source (who might have been testing you out, anyway) and the brick wall will go up. Your reliability and sincerity as a journalist are vital, and the best, biggest stories go to the journalists who reinforce these qualities with their contacts *every day*, not just when there's a story to be written. This is because big stories break outside the best efforts of spin doctors, media liaison officers and damage controllers. They break because journalists—good ones—spend a lot of time talking, working their contacts and doing the groundwork of keeping in touch.

The capacity to distinguish between relationships with contacts that compromise independence, and those that respect independence as crucial to best journalistic practice is a mark of competency. In their willingness to act on this capacity—which may sometimes involve 'burning' a contact for one of journalism's larger ethical concerns (public interest, democratic process, truth), reporters develop the more pronounced marks of commitment and integrity.

## COMMUNITY AND CULTURAL INSTITUTIONS

You can find out about everything from fêtes, festivals and exhibitions to disasters by keeping in touch with what is happening in community and cultural institutions which interact with the public.

### Emergency services

The high-powered actions of ambulance paramedics, fire officers and Special Emergency Service (SES) volunteers in dealing with the devastation caused by bushfires, cyclones and floods provide some spectacular stories. The importance of these community services also ensures an audience for stories about changes to their operations, such as 'Fire-trucks cover for Ambulance' (Bingham & Andrews, 2003).

The police deal with offences against people and property, but they also play a prominent role in many community activities such as carnivals and festivals.

Everyone can relate to stories about hospitals because we have either been admitted to one or know someone who has. As well as the big new and continuing stories on health issues, there are many related stories involving matters such as the difficulties people may have in accessing hospital facilities—for example, 'Parents Angry Over Hospital Scan Refusal' (Edmistone, 2003).

## Community institutions

Similarly, many people are interested in finding out what is happening in schools. Changes to the curriculum—a frequent education story—is the focus of the article 'School of Thought to Enter the Classroom' (Dullroy, 2003). School students' drinking and drug habits are other perennial topics, as in the feature 'Under-age, Overproof' (Hutchinson, 2003).

Presentations and live performances, public meetings launches and exhibitions can all be scheduled by libraries. One of the bigger stories about libraries was the 2003 sell-off of rare books by the New South Wales Parliamentary Library, which was reported in many news stories and features, including 'Parliamentary Books Sail' (Ellicott, 2003).

## Cultural actitivies

Museum and gallery staff have specialised knowledge and may be willing to respond to information inquiries related to their areas of knowledge in a similar way to academics in universities.

As well as reviews of their productions, stories coming out of theatres can cover changes in their personnel and direction. Major artistic differences can result in ongoing theatre stories, such as the controversy over the director's interpretation of a David Williamson play, *Heretic*, in 1996, described in the article 'Director and Playwright Trade Blows Over Claims of Heresy' (Hawkins, 1996).

## EXERCISE

Locate the nearest large hospital, museum, gallery or theatre, find a story there and write an eight-par news report about it. Who is the director of the institution? Does it produce a newsletter? Are any events or exhibitions worth a news report? Are there statistical changes to report on, for example changes in the rates of admission or attendances? Check their press releases and those issued by the relevant government department to identify any existing issues. Have any articles about this institution appeared recently and which you could follow up?

## EVENTS

Significant events which may produce good stories happen every day. While events such as accidents and emergencies are random, numerous scheduled events are organised by professional, community and cultural groups.

How do you find out where the scheduled events are? Lists of activities are available through the groups or institutions that host them. They may place newspaper ads, and their current events will appear on their websites. It is easy to subscribe to email newsletters.

You can use OnlineEvents (www.onlineevents.com.au) and the New Zealand Events Guide (www.nz-events.co.nz/

event/aboutevents.shtml) to find conferences, exhibitions, trade shows and expos.

## Groups and organisations

One-off events organised by activists, lobby or pressure groups or charities are often good story material, or lead to new story ideas. You may get a tip-off that a newsworthy event is about to take place—for instance, a phone call, email or SMS from a member of an activist group such as Amnesty International (www.amnesty.org.au/index.html) about a demonstration, public meeting or new major campaign launch.

Lobby groups such as the Australian Chamber of Commerce and Industry (www.acci.asn.au) may schedule speeches, public meetings, policy releases and campaign launches. Charities such those linked through Australian Charities (www.auscharity.org) also launch fundraising campaigns with public events.

See the listings at the Australian Sports Commission (www.ausport.com.au) for events convened by sporting groups.

## Visits and launches

For publishers' announcements about visits by well-known authors or the launch of new books, see the Events Directory at the Australian Literature Gateway (www.austlit.edu.au), Ozlit's Australian Publishers (http://home.vicnet.net.au/~ozlit) and literary events through the New Zealand Book Council (www.bookcouncil.org.nz).

## Festivals and concerts

The Music section from The Space, at ABC ArtsOnline (www.abc.net.au/arts) includes notices about festivals and concerts, while the Australia Dance Council (www.ausdance.org.au) and the AusStage: Gateway to the Australian Performing Arts (www.ausstage.edu.au) sites include events notices.

For a guide to the equivalent New Zealand events, see the Arts Calendar Guide to New Zealand Arts (www.arts calendar.co.nz). Film and community festivals feature in the Festivals & Events at LookSmart Australia (www.sensis.com. au/looksmart).

## Conferences

Conferences organised by university departments, professional groups and companies are invaluable for catching up with the latest developments, as well as for making contacts. Visitors can often attend the product presentations by vendors even if they are not formally registered at the conference.

To find academic conferences, see the Australian Vice-Chancellors' Committee (AVCC) listing of Australian universities (www.avcc.edu.au). Try the contact directory from Australian Science & Technology Online (www. asto.com.au) to find science organisations, and Business Australia (www.agd.com.au/browse/Business%20Australia) to find companies.

## Talks and exhibitions

As well as conferences, events held by university departments and research institutions include seminars and public lectures, while talks and exhibitions convened by museums and galleries are listed in the What's On listing at Australian Museums & Galleries Online (http://amol.org.au). EdNA Online (www.edna.edu.au) includes a variety of educational events.

## Government events

The public can attend parliamentary sittings and many council meetings, and committee hearings may also be open to interested visitors. Details about these events are available through the Australian Government Entry Point (www.gov.au) and the New Zealand Government's portal (www.govt.nz).

## EXERCISE

Find three events happening this week within your local community. Attend one and write a brief news story about it which would be suitable for a community newspaper.

## REGIONAL REPORTING
### Susan Hetherington

To gather the regional news successfully, you need to make and maintain a number of crucial contacts.

First, you should get to know representatives from the emergency services such as the police, ambulance and fire brigade. Police sources worth befriending include the duty sergeant, the Traffic Branch chief, the detective in charge of CIB and any friendly police officer. Court personnel such as the police prosecutor and the clerk of court are also important to know.

Your local council is packed with useful contacts. Get to know your mayor and the councillors, especially the heads of factions or the official opposition. Significant local government officials include the shire clerk and the town planner, as well as the head of the planning committee and the mayor's secretary.

While you are talking to sources or attending meetings at the council, look out for items about changes in land zonings, applications for developments and the scale of new building projects. To gauge local feeling, check the number of objections to developments and land zoning changes, as well as the number of people in the public gallery when the changes are being discussed.

Your council will be able to provide you with details of the number and value of developments they have approved—these are a good indication of the state of the local economy. Other newsworthy data include the figures for traffic accidents, vandalism and notifiable diseases.

There will be many special interest groups in your community for you to befriend, including environmental groups, Neighbourhood Watch, school parents and citizens' groups, pensioner groups, residents and rate-payers' associations as well as service clubs such as Apex and Rotary.

Things that you should be aware of will also be happening in community institutions such as schools and the local hospitals, and also in organisations such as the Chamber of Commerce and the Tourism Association.

Look out for the local implications of wider issues such as homeless people: when new statistics for the metropolitan area are released you could find out how many local homeless there are and who they are.

Is there any new legislation that affects people or businesses in your area—for example, changes to policies about class sizes which will affect the size of classes in your local school?

Don't forget to check what live arts and entertainment events are happening in town—they're a guaranteed source of stories.

## NON-PROFIT ORGANISATIONS

Does the topic or issue you are researching have an organisation, trade body or help group which is pumping out news which you could use? Keeping in touch with the activities of relevant groups through their websites, email newsletters or by having contacts within organisations will keep you informed about issues and possible stories.

These groups can be a goldmine of information and interview subjects. *Sydney Morning Herald* journalist Malcolm Brown says:

Prior to the final submissions on the HIH royal commission, I was asked to get some personal stories from victims of the HIH collapse. I did not know where to start but I did remember an activist for home buildings whose name, organisation and contact phone numbers I had put on the Contacts System and updated every two years. So I contacted her and she was delighted to give me the names and addresses of two victims, whom I interviewed. The interviews were published yesterday. I would probably not have got them if I had not invested in the in-depth contingency planning that had always struck me as essential for the operation of a newspaper. (Brown, 2003)

The range of these local and national non-profit groups includes charities, foundations, unions, lobby groups, activist groups, chambers of commerce, historical societies and fan clubs. These organisations can be political, sporting, religious or industry based, and they are often affiliated with other groups in networks. Their role can include a responsibility for educating and informing the public, so their newsletters and other publications may contain credible data.

For example, the beach drownings and rescue figures in the annual *National Surf Safety Report* from Surf Life Saving Australia are widely quoted in news reports.

Even though their goal may not be to produce a profit, organisations and associations may also be structured as a company, in which case they will be obliged to supply information to the corporate watchdogs. See Chapter 3, 'Digging up the business bones'.

## Activist and lobby groups

Activist groups such as Amnesty International (www.amnesty.org) or lobby groups such as Children by Choice (www.childrenbychoice.org.au) are excellent places to find story ideas because societal problems often show up first in these groups.

For example, a child welfare group may publicise problems experienced by children placed with foster parents. Their group's activities may result in changes to the policies governing the way that children in need are placed, and increased funding for these programs.

Big, powerful lobby groups such as the Minerals Council of Australia (www.minerals.org.au), are easy to find in the telephone book or online. NZ lobby groups can be found through Lobby Groups (http://webdirectory.natlib.govt.nz/dir/en/nz/community-and-social-studies/lobby-groups).

Smaller environmental groups may be harder to find, but they are usually part of a network such as those in GreenNet

Australia (www.green.net.au) or ECO (www.eco.org.nz). Once you find one group, it is generally easier to find others.

The documents that activist groups post to their websites can produce stories, as described in the story 'Nursing Homes Rated Unacceptable' (Israel & Vaughan, 2000) which reported that documents the Australian federal government had failed to provide had been posted to the website of a watchdog group. The reports documented nursing homes and hostels in New South Wales which had 'unacceptable aspects of operation'.

Look at the reports of parliamentary inquiries for the names and contact information of interested parties, such as organisations which made a submission to the investigation.

Philanthropy Australia (www.philanthropy.org.au/links/links.htm) contains a list of Australian foundations, while Australian Professional Organisations (www.journoz.com/ausproforgs.html) includes associations and societies.

Trade and export organisations may have research programs which produce excellent specialised information. They usually publish their own newsletters or journals, have a specialised library or information centre and can also contribute relevant statistics such as car production figures for the year.

## Trade unions

The staff of associations such as carers' associations and trade unions, which exist to advance the needs or protect the interests of a group of people, often know a lot about the institutions which employ the people they represent, and they may be prepared to share their knowledge. For instance, the officers of the New South Wales Nursing Association (www.nswnurses.asn.au) are familiar with the operations of the New South Wales Health Department. Contact unions through the ACTU National Directory On-line (www.directory.actu.asn.au) and the New Zealand Council of Trade Unions (www.union.org.nz).

In a similar way, the officers of charities and lobby groups will be familiar with the government department or statutory authority which administers the programs used by those people whose interests they represent.

Sporting groups will supply player statistics, experts and match information. For example, to find Test cricket batting averages go to the Stats Guru on Cricinfo (www.cricinfo.com), which is run by the Wisden Group, or try the Australian Cricket Board (www.abc.com.au).

Use the OzGuide listing for Organisations (www.journoz.com/orgs.html) to find groups. Non-profit organisations can also be found through directories, yearbooks and the *Yellow Pages*.

## EXERCISE

Find a story in a newsletter, report or other publication issued by a group such as a charity, trade union, sporting group or an activist group such as an environmental or human rights group working in the areas of climate change, child abuse, gay marriage, refugees or euthanasia.

Follow up by contacting one representative of this group and obtaining more information about the issue or the group's activities in this area.

Find a submission made by such a group to a committee inquiry.

## UNIVERSITIES, RESEARCH INSTITUTES AND THINK-TANKS

Academics employed by universities have a tradition of independence from influence by outside forces, and of having the right to express their opinions freely. This independence and intensive knowledge of diverse areas such as crime, science, town planning, media and economics mean that they are often called on to act as experts, analyse issues and explain the reasons for phenomena and problems.

## Academic experts

Experts with specialised qualifications can be found through the directories supplied by virtually all universities. For example, the University of Otago's site includes a searchable Expertise Database (http://policy01.otago.ac.nz/expertise/index.html). See the Australian universities directories guide (www.avcc.edu.au) to find university directories of experts. These directories usually have a search facility so you can put in a term such as 'substance abuse' to find an expert in this area.

New Zealand universities are listed in the Te Puna web directory (http://webdirectory.natlib.govt.nz/dir/en/nz/education/tertiary-education/universities).

Xpertnet, a service provided by Macquarie University's public relations sections, finds experts with knowledge of particular areas by distributing requests to media officers in universities. This service is listed as one of the university's services for journalists (www.pr.mq.edu.au/jou.htm).

## Research papers

Academics in universities and research institutes publish papers which analyse and explain social, political and economic changes and issues, and place them a in social, economic and historical context.

For example, the staff of the National Centre for Social and Economic Modelling (NATSEM) at the University of Canberra (www.natsem.canberra.edu.au) use research tools to model the social and economic effects of changes of government policy.

*Background Briefing* reporter Stan Correy (2004) uses these reports frequently. He says:

> People want information in digested form as it appears in newspapers and popular magazines, but the best information for journalists is in original materials, in research reports, in the material referred to in the footnotes in articles and papers.

Stories such as 'Misunderstood Maggots Help to Fight Crime' (King, 2003) highlight the results of research performed within research institutes—in this case the Centre for Forensic Science at the University of Western Australia.

Research performed for the Australian Council of Trade Unions (ACTU) by the staff of Royal Melbourne Institute of Technology (RMIT) and the Australian Centre for Industrial Relations Research and Training at the University of Sydney, formed the basis of the major feature 'Still Work in Progress' (Steketee, 2003). This story focused on changes to the makeup of the labour force.

## Research integrity

To perform research successfully, academics need to be able to report on their results regardless of how disturbing their findings are to powerful people and organisations. This tradition of openness means that research results produced by academics in universities or research institutes should not be affected by market forces.

However, the reports produced by this kind of research can sometimes still be affected by the expectations or constraints imposed by the commissioning agent. For instance, a company involved in marketing genetically modified (GM) food could fund a project to research this food, and the research findings could demonstrate that GM food can be consumed without any problems. The research could be perfectly sound, but it is also possible that the result has been skewed by the expectations of the funding body.

Therefore, it is important to find out which body funded the project before accepting the results of research. Information about the origin of grants may be freely available from an institute or university's website, or it may be shown in reports such as their annual report.

## Finding research and experts

Ring public relations departments in universities for help if you have heard about some interesting research being done there; they should be able to find the department or centre and the person you need to talk to.

Universities publish regular newspapers or newsletters which may yield interesting stories about the latest research developments.

University guides to their research centres include Research Centres & Units (www.otago.ac.nz/research/centres/index.html) at the University of Otago, which links to the university's centres and applied research units.

Directories of experts include the Australian Public Intellectual (API) Network (www.api-network.com/cgi-bin/page?home/index), the members of Australian Policy Online (www.apo.org.au/profiles.shtml), which includes policy centres and institutes, and the CRC Program Directory (www.crc.gov.au) which focuses on the cooperative research centres which bring together researchers from universities, government laboratories, public sector agencies and private industry.

## Theses

Theses written by postgraduate students contain the results of original research and may include research breakthroughs which arise from taking a fresh approach to old problems.

All Australian universities require at least one copy of doctoral and masters' theses to be deposited in the university library. These can be located through the library catalogues and requested from other libraries by inter-library loan.

The Australian Digital Theses (ADT) Program (http://adt. caul.edu.au) produces a database of digitised theses produced at Australian universities.

A subscription service available through libraries, Proquest Digital Dissertations, provides citations and abstracts for theses completed at universities throughout the world.

Dissertation Abstracts International is a monthly compilation of abstracts of doctoral dissertations from more than 350 institutions, mostly from the United States and Canada.

Abstracts for theses accepted for higher degrees in Great Britain and Ireland are provided through the UK Index to Theses (www.theses.com).

## Think-tanks

Think-tanks use research results to try to influence decisions about government policy. They may be a bountiful source of specialised information, expert contacts and statistics, but reporters need to keep their agenda in mind when appraising their data.

Some well-known think-tanks are The Evatt Foundation (http://evatt.labor.net.au), the Australian Strategic Policy Institute (www.aspi.org.au), The Institute of Public Affairs (www.ipa.org.au), The Sydney Institute (www.thesydney

institute.com.au/home.html) and the Australia Institute (www.tai.org.au).

Many think-tanks are funded by corporate bodies and this must be taken into consideration when assessing their information. As well as producing their own publications, they may have a library or information centre.

Reports released by think-tanks often become news. An example is 'Savings in Weaning Mums off Welfare' (Jackman, 2003b), which was based on a report released by the Centre for Independent Studies (www.cis.org.au /main/titlebar2.htm).

US Sources and Experts (http://metalab.unc.edu/ slanews/internet/experts.html) includes experts from universities, think-tanks and other organisations. NIRA's World Directory of Think Tanks (www.nira.go.jp) is a comprehensive directory of think-tanks around the world.

## EXERCISES

1 Choose a major issue in the news and find an academic expert to comment on it.
2 Find reports on a similar topic released by both a research institute and a think-tank, and compare their treatments.

# 3

## DIGGING UP THE
## BUSINESS BONES

Business journalists report on what is happening in major companies, such as changes in the lineup of executives or the appointment of a new director to the board. Business news is often about markets—for example, the stockmarket is up or down or the housing market is going through a downturn.

As well as this news, the public have a right to know about corporate misbehaviour, which includes corrupt dealings by directors and accountants where they act in their own interests rather than those of the company. Companies may hide their profits to avoid paying tax, or they may falsely claim that their company is making big profits through buying and selling their own assets. All these practices make it impossible for potential shareholders to make an accurate decision about whether to buy, sell or retain shares in the company.

## SOURCES IN ORGANISATIONS

If you are not familiar with businesses, you may wish to begin by skimming through the information in the section below on 'Companies'. If you already understand these structures, this section also contains suggestions about some tools to use when you are researching in the business area.

To find out what's happening in business, begin to make and keep contacts inside and outside of corporations, and amongst regulators, professional organisations and lobby groups. Keep in touch with what's happening by going to events such as trade shows and shareholders' meetings and chatting with people who could become your contacts.

Companies provide information through their own publications, such as their newsletters, annual reports and websites. Check their sites, such as the Foster's Group's site (www.fosters.com.au/corporate) for links to their press releases, notices about upcoming meetings and events, and speeches by their chairperson or CEO.

Company annual reports should include the principal company activities, profit and loss performance, reports from the directors, CEO and chairman of the board, balance sheet and notification of new ventures.

For a basic introduction to reading financial statements, see the IBM Guide to financials at www.prars.com/ibm/ibmframe.html.

Major banks and stockbrokers such as Commonwealth Securities Ltd (www.comsec.com.au) provide information about daily currency rates and listed companies. You can compare currency rates over time through Oz Forex Foreign Exchange (www.ozforex.com.au).

Market research reports on business trends describe the current state, history, competitors and future of particular industries. These studies are available for a fee; the firms which produce them may make excerpts or summaries available for free on their websites. MarketResearch.com (www.marketresearch.com) offers reports under industry sectors.

Non-profit organisations, such as the industry association the Minerals Council of Australia (MCA) (www.minerals.

org.au) produce publications such as the MCA's *Monthly Minerals Update*.

Lobby groups and industry representatives may make submissions to parliamentary committees investigating current issues. These submissions can provide the background for stories about serious problems within industries, such as the HIH Royal Commission Submission on Future Policy Directions which can be found at www.hihroyalcom.gov.au/FuturePolicy/submit.asp. This report provided material for stories about the inadequacies in the prudential regulation of the insurance industry.

Unions, churches, charities and social justice organisations may provide their own research services. For example, the Labor Council of New South Wales' Bosswatch (www.bosswatch.labor.net.au) collects information about companies, their interrelationships and working conditions. You can find other unions through the Australian Council of Trade Unions (ACTU) (www.actu.asn.au) and the New Zealand Council of Trade Unions (CTU) (www.union.org.nz).

Intra-governmental organisations such as the International Monetary Fund (IMF) provide copious amounts of information. The World Bank Group, (www.worldbank.org) has excellent country-specific information and country economic forecasts.

The research papers produced by universities, research units and think-tanks may be published in journals, or provided through the organisation, for example, the Asia Pacific Press Online Working Papers (http://ncdsnet. anu.edu.au/online/workpaper.htm).

A typical example of a story obtained from a research report is 'Company Donations Heavily Favour Libs' (Dodson, 2000), which was based on a research report from the Centre for Corporate Law and Securities Regulation at the University of Melbourne.

## Government agencies: researchers, regulators and watchdogs

Government departments and statutory authorities such as the Reserve Bank of Australia (www.rba.gov.au) and the Reserve Bank of New Zealand (www.rbnz.govt.nz) produce data and research reports on industries, markets, economic indicators, business conditions and regional development.

The Australian Bureau of Agriculture and Resource Economics (ABARE) (www.affa.gov.au) provides policy analysis and forecasts relevant to Australia's agricultural and resource industries.

You can check the name of a business through the Australian Business Register (http://abr.business.gov.au), and obtain their Australian Company Number (ACN) or Australian Registered Body Number (ARBN), which can make it easier to obtain further information about the company.

Businesses register their trademarks through each state's Australian Industrial Property Organisation (AIPO) (www.aipo.gov.au) office, which maintains the Trade Marks Office database (www.ipaustralia.gov.au).

The databases of registered business names are available for public scrutiny through the departments which maintain them, such as state departments of Consumer Affairs and Fair Trading, as well as the Australian Securities and Investments Commission (ASIC) for the businesses which are registered there. You can search ASIC online for free to check a business name. Business names are held at the following offices:

- NSW  Office of Fair Trading (www.fair-trading.nsw.gov. au/business.html);
- ACT  Registrar General's Office (www.rgo.act.gov.au);
- VIC  Victorian Names Register, Consumer Affairs (www.consumer.vic.gov.au);

- SA    Office of Consumer & Business Affair (www.ocba. ca.gov.au);
- WA    Business Names, Consumer & Employment Protection (www.docep.wa.gov.au);
- NT    Department of Justice (www.nt.gov.au/justice);
- QLD   Office of Fair Trading (www.fairtrading. qld.gov.au);
- TAS   Consumer Affairs & Fair Trading (www.justice.tas. gov.au/newca/index.htm);
- NZ    The New Zealand Companies Office (www. companies.govt.nz).

The Australian Competition and Consumer Commission (ACCC) (www.accc.gov.au) investigates business and trade practices for anti-competitive behaviour.

In New Zealand, the Securities Commission (www.seccom.govt.nz) regulates capital markets. The New Zealand Commerce Commission (www.comcom.govt.nz) is responsible for fair trading and consumer information.

The Insolvency and Trustee Service Australia (ITSA) (www.itsa.gov.au) operates the bankruptcy registry, or National Personal Insolvency Index, where public records on insolvency are maintained.

The Australian Prudential Regulation Authority (www. apra.gov.au) is responsible for the prudential regulation of banking institutions, insurers, friendly societies and superannuation funds.

In New Zealand, the Companies Office (www.companies. govt.nz) of the Ministry of Economic Development registers corporate bodies.

## The corporate watchdogs

You can research what's happening within business through accessing the records kept by the corporate watchdogs. Basic company information is freely available from their shop-fronts or through their websites, while more complex information is available for a fee.

To trade their shares, companies must be listed with the Australian Stock Exchange (ASX) (www.asx.com.au) and supply information to the ASX.

As well as overseeing share trading, the ASX provides information to investors and the public about the activities of listed companies.

Companies trading shares in New Zealand operate in accordance with the requirements of the New Zealand Stock Exchange (www.nzse.co.nz), while the US Securities and Exchange Commission (www.sec.gov) covers US stock trading.

Australian companies and trading bodies should be registered with the Australian Securities and Investment Commission (ASIC) (www.asic.gov.au). ASIC's function is to protect those intending to do business with, or invest in, registered companies by enforcing the Corporations Law against problems such as breaches of directors' duties.

The information which is available for free from the ASIC includes the current and former name of a company or trust, its Australian Company Number (CAN), Body Number (ARBN) or Registration Number, the kind of entity it is and whether it has lodged accounts.

The path to this information is: www.asic.gov.au -> 'Search' -> 'National Names Index'.

ASIC charges a fee for searches of its databases performed through its Service Centres or by paying an information broker such as the CITEC Confirm service (wwww.confirm.com.au) and Connect4 (www.connect4.com.au).

The searches available through the ASIC databases include:

- personal name searches, which focus on an individual's interests and activities, and show the companies that individual is connected with;
- company extracts, which produce lists of organisations' directors, the principal officers, the type of company, the registered office and shareholder information;
- an historical search, which adds the names of previous directors and shareholders and their addresses, when the directors or company secretary changed, or when shareholders bought in or sold out. This sort of information can illuminate connections between individuals, businesses and public officials such as local government councillors;
- a relational company extract, which shows the roles the company plays in other organisations. This could show the other companies it owns or is involved with. Public companies often have many subsidiaries, and finding out who actually controls a company can involve searching back through many layers of shelf companies;
- the registers of professional directors and disqualified directors;
- the registers of licensed trades and professions; and
- the docu-images of documents lodged with the ASIC, such as company returns, which show the number of people the organisation has sacked and their profits during a given time.

## COMPANIES

To research business, it helps to understand some of the main business structures, which are explained below.

A company is an association of people formed to conduct business or other activities in the name of the association. Lobby groups, clubs, housing associations, professional practices and individuals can all be registered companies.

A company may begin as a private company and then, after the directors have built it up, be listed as a public company, with shares being sold to make a profit. Or a former public entity such as Telstra may be privatised by being turned into a company whose shares are then sold to the public.

## Public companies

Public companies have 'Limited' after their name, have their shares listed on the Stock Exchange for trading and must appoint an auditor. To trade shares, companies must have 300 or more shareholders; need to have made an operating profit before tax for the past three years of $500 000 per year; or have net tangible assets of $5 million.

Public companies are obliged to keep the market informed about changes that might affect people's decisions to buy or sell shares. For instance, before a share issue, they must issue a prospectus which explains how the company intends using the capital raised by selling the shares. They must comply with disclosure requirements set by the corporate watchdogs, which then have a responsibility to make this information available to the public.

## Private companies

Private companies have 'Proprietary Limited' after their name. These companies are often set up by small business people; they have a limited number of shares which are not available for trading by the public. About 90 per cent of the companies in Australia are private companies. The structure of a private company protects the directors from personal liability, so that people owed money by the company cannot access directors' personal assets.

Small private companies with a gross revenue of less than $10 million; gross assets less than $5 million; and fewer than 50 employees are generally not obliged to submit financial statements to the corporate regulators. These 'exempt class' companies make up about 95 per cent of private companies. 'Non-exempt' private companies do have to lodge accounts, and may be audited.

*Unlisted public companies* are obliged to lodge annual accounts, although they operate as private companies. They can be mutual organisations which are privately owned by their policy holders, and they can act as trustees, keeping funds on others' behalf.

## No liability, limited and unlimited liability

No liability companies are usually speculative, and are often mining or oil companies. They and their directors are not liable for shareholders' losses.

Companies limited by guarantee may be football clubs, foundations and charities. These not-for-profit limited companies have members who are not liable for company debts. They are run under rules of association set by state government offices of Corporate Affairs or Fair Trading. From them, you should be able to find out some financial details about the association, and who is running it.

The directors of unlimited liability companies, which are often insurance companies, are personally liable for the company's debts.

## Intermediary and loophole companies

*Nominee companies* can be used as intermediaries, to set up companies which separate individuals from the companies in which they have an interest. *Holding companies* provide a loophole to shelter the activities of subsidiary companies under one entity so that the subsidiaries are not obliged to provide financial information to the public.

## Trusts

Trusts involve a person or entity taking charge of property owned by another person or entity, in order to benefit the owner or beneficiary.

*Property trusts* may be listed on the Stock Exchange, so information about them should be available. If they are unlisted, a prospectus may still be available from the company. *Cash management trusts* pool small investments, and fixed trusts are those in which investors have fixed entitlements at all times.

*Family trusts* may be used to store wealth if any of the companies with which the family is involved should decline; these are difficult for journalists to investigate.

## Liquidation

The directors who control a company may decide to pay their debts and wind the company up, or a creditor may call a meeting of the company's creditors and suggest liquidating the company to sell its assets. This is called a 'creditors' voluntary liquidation'.

If a creditor serves an unsuccessful notice to pay on a company, and then gets a court order to liquidate a company, a 'court-ordered liquidation' results and a copy of the statement of claim lodged within the court should be available to journalists. The reports to the court made by the liquidator who takes control of the company should also be available. A company may elect to go into receivership, or a creditor may get a court order to appoint a receiver, who then runs the company.

When individuals or companies are declared bankrupt, a large amount of information about their business dealings is made available to the courts, and this may also be made available to the public.

## EXERCISES

1   Find a current business story in this week's newspapers that involves a conflict of interest. Use public record sources such as records of parliamentary debates to develop a fresh angle on this story that also incorporates new developments.
2   What are Australia's or New Zealand's top five public companies? Find the names of their chairperson, board members and CEO.
3   Find a recent newsletter or report produced by the Reserve Bank or Treasury which contains an announcement of a new policy or a policy changed which will affect individuals, households, the finance industry, the service industry or manufacturers. Write a news story about the change that contains a response from a representative of the group/s affected by the new policy.

# 4

## SNIFFING THE LEGAL BREEZE

There are payoffs for researchers who make the effort to come to grips with the law.

If you are working on stories about changes to the building codes, suspected corruption, development disputes or access to nursing home beds, it may help to read the relevant Act or case yourself. You could be keen to find out whether an action is a crime in the terms of one of the *Crimes Acts*, or you might need to find out the normal level of damages in certain types of cases.

Lawyers who are often rung by journalists say they would prefer to comment rather than supply basic briefings about legislation which is freely available for anyone to read. However, it can be difficult for laypeople to understand legislation (also called Acts or statutes), and misinterpreting an Act could lead to unfortunate consequences, such as an expensive defamation action.

After reading the legislation, it would be wise to check with a lawyer to confirm that you have understood correctly its meaning, its interpretation by the courts, and the significance of any amendments.

A brief explanation follows about the structure and creation of legislation, with some pointers about where to find Acts.

# LEGAL INFORMATION

## Primary and secondary legal materials

Primary legal materials include the Acts passed by parliament, the rules, regulations and by-laws passed by authoritative bodies, and the reports of the decisions of the courts.

As well as the primary materials, many secondary materials describe and explain the law, and resources such as legal textbooks, encyclopaedias and dictionaries may be easier for people without legal training to understand. The tools which researchers can use to find and comprehend the law include digests, newsletters, journals, legal commentaries and current awareness services.

## The creation of law

Law is created by parliament passing legislation which becomes an Act of Parliament; it is also created when amendments to Acts are passed. Law is also made within the courts when judges make decisions about how to interpret the words of an Act.

What this means is that, apart from the words of an Act and any amendments to it, an Act's significance depends on how its words have been interpreted by the courts in cases which depend on that Act. However, legislation overrides case law.

Any regulations which have been passed about its interpretation will also affect the effectiveness of legislation. Regulations are rules which specify how to carry out the law, and proposing new regulations can provoke stories such as 'Law Goes Soft on Financial Hard Sell' (O'Loughlin, 2002), in the *Sydney Morning Herald*, which reported that the effectiveness of the *Financial Services Reform Act 2001* could be limited by proposed regulations.

## Consolidations and Codes

Consolidating Acts may be passed to simplify matters when an Act has been extensively amended. The new statute pulls together the law on that subject as a single Act.

A Code also recreates the provisions of the existing legislation on a subject, combining this with the existing case law.

## Structure of statutes

Statutes or acts usually contain a number of sections, which can include:

- a short title and a long title;
- numbering with a serial number and the calendar year;
- a preamble, including a statement of reasons for the Act;
- an enabling part setting out what the legislation has enacted as law; and
- numbered sections which may be grouped into parts and divisions.

Check the headings of an act to get a feeling for its significance.

## Citing legislation

Legislation is cited in the following manner:

- *Pharmacists Act 1991* (SA);
- *Crimes Act 1900;*
- *Maritime Transport Security Act 2003*, s 18(1); or
- Supreme Court Rules 1970, Pt 24, r 12.

## Finding Acts of parliament

The Australasian Legal Information Institute (www.austlii. edu.au) contains Australian legislation. Other helpful portals include Federal Parliament (www.aph.gov.au), FindLaw Australia (www.findlaw.com.au) and the LawPORTAL (www.lawportal.com.au).

To find an Act through Austlii, select the category from the home page (for example, Commonwealth Consolidated Acts) and type the phrase from the act you need—for example, 'migration review'—in the search box. This search retrieves the full text of the *Migration Reform Act 1992*.

Legal information online is provided by the Law and Justice Foundation of New South Wales (www.lawfoundation.net.au).

Sources of New Zealand legislation include the government sites, New Zealand Legislation (www.legislation.govt.nz) and the parliamentary sites New Zealand legislation (www.pco.parliament.govt.nz/legislation/legislationtypes.shtml) and New Zealand Parliament (www.parliament.govt.nz).

The Knowledge Basket (http://rangi.knowledge-basket.co.nz/gpacts/actlists.html) and Legislation Direct (www.gplegislation.co.nz/acts.html) also contain Acts and regulations.

For international sources of legislation, see the Guide to Foreign and International Legal Databases (www.law.nyu.edu/library/foreign_intl/index.html) from the New York University School of Law, International Law (www.un.org/law) from the United Nations, Amnesty International (www.amnesty.org) and the International Court of Justice (www.icj-cij.org).

## EXERCISE

Find the Act which created Australia's first private university.

## COURTS AND LAWYERS

The courts are generous to journalists and writers because the dramas, dashed dreams, intrigues and controversies that are played out in court rooms each day are a bubbling well-spring of ideas, stories and research opportunities.

Most court reports that are published are about matters in the Magistrates Court, where many juicy small cases involve colourful people in trouble, or where serious criminal cases begin with committal hearings.

*Courier-Mail* investigative journalist Hedley Thomas (2003) says:

> Some story ideas come from intuition about something, for instance from seeing a two-par article in a newspaper that looks interesting and following up on it. It isn't just a matter of reading articles in newspapers though but of reading the court lists as well, especially the civil cases which are rarely if ever reported.
>
> The kind of thing I might see that could look interesting is a civil case between a private person and a government agency—for instance, the Queensland Housing Commission is suing someone. Now why would the Queensland Housing Commission be suing someone? There could be a story there.
>
> I use the E-Courts (www.ecourts.courts.qld.gov.au) facility to check when the case was first filed, then I go to the court and ask to see the files. And I read civil judgments. That was how I discovered the Baker Johnson Lawyers story [a series of stories in *The Courier-Mail* which described allegations of fraud and misrepresentation against Baker Johnson Lawyers by their client, resulting in a government inquiry into the Queensland Law Society's conduct and leading to the body being stripped by the Attorney-General of its role as a regulator of its solicitor members], through noticing that a legal firm had sued one of its former clients in the

District Court and that the judgment had gone against them. Through checking back in the Magistrates Court and the District Court, I discovered many similar cases where this same firm of lawyers had sued their former clients.

The court records that I was looking at are available to anyone. For a big story we might spend $600 or $700 on search fees but the search fees for a single case are only $10 or so.

## Court hierarchy

The hierarchy of courts leads up to the High Court, and lower courts accept the implications of the precedents set when decisions are made by the courts which are superior to them in the hierarchy. From highest down to lowest, the court hierarchy is as follows:

High Court
Federal Court
Supreme Courts
District Courts/County Courts
Magistrates Courts/Local Courts
Tribunals

Magistrates Courts or Local Courts decide simple matters or, at committal hearings, decide whether there is a case to answer in the higher courts with respect to more complex matters. A magistrate can hear and decide a summary criminal matter. For an indictable criminal charge—meaning that the matter will need to be decided by a jury—a magistrate can decide whether to take the matter further at a committal hearing.

Children's Courts and Coroner's Courts operate similarly to Magistrates/Local Courts.

The next level of courts is District Courts (known as County Courts in Victoria). District Courts hear cases involving charges such as assault, armed robbery, supplying drugs and the lower categories of sexual assault.

The Supreme Court heads each state judicial system. These courts hear cases involving serious crimes such as murder, arson and the higher categories of sexual assault.

Federal Courts hear matters involving more than one state, matters relating to federal laws or constitutional matters.

The general court hierarchy at Commonwealth and state levels specifies that an appeal against a decision made at a Magistrates or Lower Court goes to a District Court. An appeal against a decision made by a District Court goes to the Supreme Court, then an appeal goes to the High Court of Australia.

An appeal against a case decided by a single judge of the Supreme Court goes to the Full Court of the State Supreme Court sitting in its 'appellate jurisdiction', then to the High Court.

Administrative Tribunals resolve disputes between private parties and between private parties and government agencies—for instance, small claims tribunals and residential tenancies tribunals.

## Court reporting

For justice to be seen to be done, the courts need to be open to scrutiny by the public—although there are exceptions to this rule, such as the hearings of the Family Court and Children's Courts in some states. The need for public scrutiny means that members of the public can attend most court hearings, and information about the decisions of the courts is available on the public record.

To find out which cases are being heard in which courts, use the court lists which set out the cases to be heard. These are published in newspapers, on the lists in the registry office of courthouses, online through the court sites and through the police and the prosecutor's office. It is also wise to check published accounts of previous appearances.

Court lists are available through the FindLaw portal (www.findlaw.com.au), under the Daily Court and Tribunal listing. Another section, Court Information, also contains information about the courts. The New Zealand courts can be found through the Ministry of Law (www.courts.govt.nz).

## Civil and criminal actions

A *civil* case is one where a citizen (the plaintiff) initiates a legal action against another citizen (the defendant).

A *criminal* case is one where the police (the prosecutors) take action against a citizen (the accused) regarding an offence against the state. These cases may be 'summary', meaning that a magistrate may hear them and make a decision, or 'indictable', meaning that the matter will go to a trial.

There are differences between the different states as to the aspects of court proceedings you can report on, but some general principles apply.

Journalists do not have a legal right to any greater privileges in court than the general public, although in most cases they are allowed to take notes. Approach the Clerk of the Court if you need to ask for anything in court.

To avoid the possibility of a defamation action, court reports must be fair and accurate. Only basic information about the case can be published in the period between when someone is charged and when their case is heard. You can generally publish reports of what is said in open court or tendered to the magistrate or judge, as long as your report is fair and accurate.

In a criminal case, you can usually report the charge and when the offence occurred, the parties' names; their details; the plea, if one is entered; and the court's finding, including where and when the case has been adjourned to. The magistrate or judge, the prosecutor and the defence counsel may also be identified. The witnesses may be identified with their addresses (without house numbers).

Evidence is usually 'alleged' and should be balanced with denials. Evidence presented to committal hearings is not reported.

Once they have been charged with serious offences, the accused may be given bail, which means they pay a bond to be allowed to leave; or they may be remanded, which means they stay in gaol until their trial.

Under the 'sub judice' rules which are part of the law of contempt, material which is likely to prejudice the conduct or outcome of a matter before the courts, usually in a jury trial, cannot be published.

You must never prejudge cases by describing someone as guilty or innocent before the court decides this, or publish their criminal record before they are convicted or acquitted. In addition, you must not publish material that has not been given in open court, or any withdrawn questions.

In some states, the victims of sexual offences must not be identified in any way; nor should the accused be identified until they have been committed for trial, and not then if it will identify the victim.

Children who appear in children's courts or in other courts must never be identified, regardless of whether they are victims, accused or witnesses. And none of the people who appear in the Family Court should be identified.

Much care needs to be taken when reporting suicide

cases, crimes with a public safety element and those involving minority groups.

## Court records

Useful contacts for obtaining court records and files include people within the prosecutor's office, the police and the staff of the registry office of the courthouse.

What is publicly available varies from state to state. Court files will usually be provided unless an order has been made to suppress them. Registry offices may be able to supply lists of cases concerning particular people or companies.

Documents include the summary and charge sheets, the statements of facts and transcripts from court houses. These documents can only be used if they have been read in court.

Wills lodged for 'probate'—which means the will is validated and executors are authorised—are available to the public through the Supreme Court's Probate Registry.

## Case law

Case law is made as the courts make decisions, and courts usually treat decisions of previous cases as precedents. However, case law can always be overridden by legislation.

Acts of parliament, which are also known as legislation or statutes, are created by parliaments, but the judges in courts have the power to create common law by interpreting Acts, and by passing opinion on legal principles in their decisions.

## Reported decisions

From the thousands of cases heard in Australian courts, law reports are written about the small minority of cases where the case is decided by a judge or judges, and the judgment of the case establishes significant legal points.

Collections of law reports may include cases decided by a particular court, or courts of a certain jurisdiction, or cases collected on a geographical basis or by topic.

Law reports may be found in library catalogues or online under their title, such as 'Commonwealth Law Reports' or under their jurisdiction and the relevant court, such as 'Victoria, District Court'.

Law libraries staffed by law librarians who can assist with finding law reports can be located through the Australian Libraries Gateway (www.nla.gov.au/apps/libraries).

Law reports can be found online through the Australasian Legal Information Institute (www.austlii.edu. au), FindLaw Australia (www.findlaw.com.au) and the LawPORTAL (www.lawportal.com.au).

Sources of New Zealand law reports include The Knowledge Basket (http://rangi.knowledge-basket.co.nz/gpacts/actlists.html). KIWINET, which is produced by the National Library of New Zealand, contains full texts of Court of Appeal judgments.

## Unreported decisions

If a case is not reported, only the judgment of the case is in the public domain, apart from Family Law and Children's Court cases.

If the case in which are interested has not been reported, you may be able to find the judgment and any written decisions either from unreported judgments services, from court registries for a fee, or through the court's website.

Austlii includes judgments from most courts in its Austlii Documents Collections (www.austlii.edu.au/databases. html#cth), as well as the judgments made by entities such as the Press Council.

## Elements of a case citation

Cases are named after the parties to the dispute, usually printed in italics: *Plaintiff v Defendant*; *Appellant v Respondent.*

The elements of citations usually appear in this order: Parties; year the decision was delivered; volume number of law report series; report series abbreviation; page number of first page of report—for example, *Johnson v Bones* [1970] 1 NSWR 28. This case was reported at page 28 of volume 1 of *The New South Wales Reports* for 1970.

In a civil matter, the parties are described as *plaintiff* (aggrieved person) *v defendant* (alleged wrongdoer).

When the plaintiff in a civil matter loses the case and decides to appeal the decision, the people involved appear as: *appellant* (plaintiff) *v respondent* (defendant). When the defendant loses but is allowed to appeal, the people appear as: *respondent* (plaintiff) *v appellant* (defendant).

## Finding lawyers

You can find lawyers to consult through centres such as the Arts Law Centre (www.artslaw.com.au), the Communications Law Centre (www.comslaw.org.au), the Copyright Centre (www.copyright.org.au) for copyright issues, a Community Legal Centre (www.worldlii.org/catalog/2529.html), the law societies in each state and the Law and Justice Foundation of New South Wales (www.lawfoundation.net.au).

## EXERCISE

Attend a hearing of the nearest Magistrates Court and write an eight-par news story about one of the cases you heard there.

# 5

# TRACKING DOWN GOVERNMENT RESOURCES

## PARLIAMENTS AND GOVERNMENT

Before you start foraging through the highways and byways of government bodies to track down information, you need a basic understanding of how the system works. This brief description outlines the activities of the different sections of government and the organisations that exist to carry out these responsibilities.

In 1901, a federation of six states formed the Commonwealth of Australia. The states, along with the three self-governing territories, have their own constitutions, governments and laws. There are three tiers of government in Australia: federal, state and local.

The Commonwealth Constitution sets out the matters on which the Commonwealth parliament has exclusive power to make laws. The Commonwealth can legislate over areas of broad national responsibility such as defence, foreign affairs, the economy and the monetary system, as well as federal taxation and overseas trade. The Commonwealth government also has varying powers over the territories.

The states' responsibilities include education, transport systems, police and hospitals. The state parliaments may also legislate on matters on which the Commonwealth parliament may make laws, but the federal law prevails on these, subject to a ruling by the High Court of Australia.

The Constitution can be amended either by a majority of people nationally, and in a majority of states, supporting a particular change at a referendum, or by the states unanimously handing over the power.

Australia is a constitutional monarchy. For the Commonwealth, the Governor-General of Australia is the head of state and represents the Crown, with powers delegated from the Queen. In each state, a Governor is the head of state, and also represents the Crown.

The system of government in Australia is based on the Westminster system, in which the 'separation of powers' principle means the three branches of government should operate separately. The three branches of government are:

- *parliament*, which has the legislative power to make laws;
- *the executive*, which implements the legislation; and
- *the judiciary*, which interprets and applies laws.

Laws may be made by all three levels of government—local, state and federal. Legislation can originate in the lower or upper houses of federal and state parliaments.

The lower house of the parliament of Australia, the House of Representatives, represents the voters of Australia. Its 150 members are elected on a population basis, from electorates based on districts. Members of the House of Representatives are elected for three-year terms.

The Senate, or the upper house, represents the states. The 76 senators comprise twelve elected from each of the six states, and two each from the Australian Capital Territory and the Northern Territory. State senators are elected for six-year terms, with territory senators appointed for three-year terms.

After a federal election the political party which wins the majority of seats takes office as the governing party. Its leader becomes the prime minister, and the ministers who make up the executive government are appointed from its members of parliament. Senior government ministers are members of cabinet, the main decision-making body.

Each minister is responsible for the management of particular areas or portfolios, such as foreign affairs or health. Government departments administer the Acts of Parliament which are their minister's responsibility, and report to their ministers, who are then answerable to parliament for the performance of their departments. Ministers also have some control over statutory corporations and semi-autonomous authorities.

The opposition is formed from the party with the most non-government members in the House of Representatives.

While the Commonwealth government is led by the prime minister, premiers lead state governments, and territory governments are headed by chief ministers.

## More information

More information about government in Australia is available from the House of Representatives infosheet *The Australian System of Government* (www.aph.gov.au/house) while the New Zealand system is described in *Find Information About Our System of Government* (www.govt.nz/en/aboutnz).

*Parliament: An Overview* (www.aph.gov.au/parl.htm) provides a summary of details about Australian parliament, while the *Parliamentary Handbook of the Commonwealth of Australia* (www.aph.gov.au/library/handbook) is an authoritative source of information.

## PARLIAMENT AND POLITICIANS

Political journalists are not the only hounds sniffing around parliament looking for gossip and good stories; many seekers of facts and insights find parliament a fertile hunting ground.

Parliament is more than politicians, and there is more to politicians than parliament—newsworthy and entertaining though their performances there may be.

Speeches delivered to parliament may contain important information about everything from wedding celebrants to the wine industry. The replies to questions on notice can include vital pieces of information, as can reports produced from committee hearings and inquiries.

The staff of politicians can be excellent contacts, as they tend to know a great deal about what is happening behind the scenes. Backbenchers (MPs who are not ministers or opposition spokespeople) may be more eager to talk to writers than frontbenchers (those with a portfolio).

Most ministers and many politicians will have their own websites, such as New South Wales MLA Lee Rhiannon's site (www.lee.greens.org.au), with contact information, policies, press releases and other material.

### Finding politicians

To track down politicians, use a directory such as The Commonwealth Government On-line Directory (www.gold.gov.au), Australian Parliaments, ABC Public Record (www.abc.net.au/news/politics) or *The Parliamentary Handbook of the Commonwealth of Australia* (www.aph. gov.au/library/handbook/index.htm). State- and New Zealand-based directories of members are listed below:

- Members of the Parliament of New South Wales: www.parliament.nsw.gov.au/prod/web/phweb.nsf/frames/members;
- Members of Parliament, Parliament of Victoria: www.parliament.vic.gov.au/mps.html;
- Members of the Legislative Assembly of Queensland: www.parliament.qld.gov.au/Parlib/Members;
- Current members, Parliament of Western Australia: www.parliament.wa.gov.au/web/newwebparl.nsf/iframe webpages/members+-+current;
- Members, Parliament of South Australia: www.parliament.sa.gov.au/members/7_members.shtm;
- Members, Parliament of Tasmania: www.parliament.tas.gov.au;
- MPs and members, House of Representatives, New Zealand Parliament: www.parliament.govt.nz/mps-and-ministers.html.

## Finding parliaments

State- and New Zealand-based parliament sites are listed below:
- Legislative Assembly for the Australian Capital Territory: www.legassembly.act.gov.au;
- New South Wales Parliament: www.parliament.nsw.gov.au;
- New Zealand Parliament: www.parliament.govt.nz;
- Northern Territory Legislative Assembly: www.nt.gov.au/lant;
- Parliament of South Australia: www.parliament.sa.gov.au;
- Parliament of Tasmania: www.parliament.tas.gov.au;
- Parliament of Victoria: www.parliament.vic.gov.au/default.htm;

- Parliament of Western Australia: www.parliament.wa.gov.au;
- Queensland Parliament: www.parliament.qld.gov.au.

## Press releases

Ministers—senior politicians who are responsible for particular areas such as health—have press secretaries whose job is to answer queries and circulate press releases about policies and upcoming legislation. Media Releases, Commonwealth of Australia (http://media.fed.gov.au) collects press releases from federal parliamentarians, while state parliaments have similar collections, such as the Queensland Ministerial Media Statements (http://statements.cabinet.qld.gov.au). Find New Zealand ministers' sites through Ministers, New Zealand Government (www.beehive.govt.nz/ministerlist.cfm).

## Sitting schedules

Parliaments sit for only part of each year, so it is wise to consult their sitting schedules to see whether the legislature is operating, or is in recess. These schedules are available through Live broadcasting, Parliament of Australia (www.aph.gov.au/live/webcast2.asp), The House at Work (www.aph.gov.au/house/work/index.htm) and Sittings of Parliament, New Zealand House of Representatives (www.clerk.parliament.govt.nz/Programme/Sits).

## *Hansard*: The Parliamentary Debates

Parliament may not be sitting, but you can still background past and present issues by checking in *Hansard* to find out who said what and when they said it during debates in parliament. As well as being the transcript record of debates,

*Hansard* also records proceedings and what was said to parliamentary committees.

Journalist Alan Ramsay (1999) has a long record of demonstrating government duplicity and mismanagement by using *Hansard* to report on what is said in parliament. For example, in his *Sydney Morning Herald* column 'Timor: A Debt Dishonoured' he used the record to identify speeches which went against the government line in a particular debate.

The House of Representatives and the Senate *Weekly Hansard* are available online through parliament websites (www.aph.gov.au/thisweek/hansard.htm), and also at libraries.

## Privilege

'Parliamentary privilege' applies to the proceedings of parliament, and means that members cannot be sued or prosecuted for things they said during a debate in parliament. It is meant to ensure freedom of speech in parliament.

'Absolute privilege' applies to authorised records of the proceedings of parliament, including what is said during debates in the House, and tabled documents, meaning that no action may be taken even if a statement is made with malice. The same protection applies to the statements made by witnesses to parliamentary committees.

'Qualified privilege' applies to reports of what is said and tabled in parliament. This means that what is said can be quoted in published reports, with protection from the usual legal restrictions on reporting, provided certain conditions are fulfilled—for example, if there is no malice in the reporting, and if what is quoted is accurate, fair and reasonable.

This protection enabled the *Sydney Morning Herald* to identify a man named in parliament as a 'sex slave trader' linked with spending huge sums at a casino (Murphy, 2000).

## Searching *Hansard*

To find what has been said that contains the words 'racial vilification' at the Parliament of Australia site at (http://parlinfoweb.aph.gov.au/piweb/search_main.aspx), type in keywords or the phrase 'racial vilification' and restrict your search to 'The Chambers'. (The Chambers collection includes the databases for *Hansard*, Daily Programs, Notice Papers, Journals, etc. from the House of Representatives and the Senate.) Searches can be limited by date and search terms can be combined using the Boolean operators AND, OR and NOT to make your queries more precise.

## Journals of the Senate, Votes and proceedings

While *Hansard* is the transcript of what is actually said, the official records of the houses of federal parliament are the *Journals of the Senate* and the *Votes and Proceedings* (House of Representatives) (www.aph.gov.au/house/pubs/index.htm). These day-to-day records include lists of members, registers of Bills, records of divisions, addresses, and orders for papers, notices of questions and motions.

Official records of state houses of parliament have several names—either *Minutes, Votes and Proceedings* or *Proceedings*.

## Green and white papers

Green papers, such as *AusLink: Towards the National Land Transport Plan* (www.dotars.gov.au/auslink/green_paper/greenpaper.htm) may be issued by the government during the process of making policy. They invite the public to respond to ideas about possible strategies and options for tackling current problems or issues.

White papers are statements of government policy on significant matters, which are issued to supply the public with details about proposed legislation. For example, *Advancing the National Interest* (www.dfat.gov.au/ani) was a white paper on Australia's foreign and trade policy.

## From Bills to Acts

When a new law is passed, it may drastically change people's lives—from their income, who they can marry and where they can live, down to details like how far they must build their house from their fence. For this reason, the passage of legislation from Bills to Acts is newsworthy, and longer articles may explore why a new Act was introduced and what its effects will be on the hapless public.

Bills are proposed statutes that have yet to be passed by parliament. They become Acts or enacted laws once they have passed through both houses of parliament and been given assent. To make a statute, the relevant minister brings the proposal before cabinet for approval, after which the Bill is drafted.

Unless the Bill is a money Bill, it proceeds through one of the houses of parliament in three main stages:

- The Bill is introduced, and a date fixed for debate.
- At the second reading, the minister explains the effect of the Bill. The main principles are also discussed during the second reading debate. The House may refer the Bill to a standing or select committee, when amendments may be proposed and voted on during the Consideration in Detail stage.
- The Bill is accepted as it has emerged from the committee stage at the third reading, and transmitted to the other house.

After a Bill has been passed by both houses, it is then presented to the Governor-General for royal assent.

It can then come into force on the date of assent, at a date indicated within the Act, or after the set period of time as stated in the *Acts Interpretation Act*.

To understand the significance of legislation, you could look at the wording of the original Bill, the debates as it went through parliament and any amendments. Ring civil liberties organisations such as the Council of Civil Liberties, or law academics, to keep tabs on the implication of new Bills, and check on reports from committees such as the Senate Scrutiny of Bills Committee.

You can track the progress of Bills through parliament through sites such as Parliament of Australia—Bills (www.aph.gov.au/bills/index.htm), which contains current and daily Bills, and Bills digests, or summaries of Bills, which explain them in simple terms.

New Zealand Bills can be tracked through Progress of Bills, New Zealand Parliament (www.clerk.parliament.govt. nz/Publications).

## Parliamentary libraries

Parliamentary libraries produce their own publications, which contain high-quality research prepared for ministers and members of parliament in the form of research reports, Bills Digests (www.clerk.parliament.govt.nz/Publications/ ResearchPapers), current awareness services and economic and social statistics.

Their research reports are often available on their websites or in state and university libraries. They are used by journalists to produce stories such as 'A New Rule Book for Our Politicians?' (Wainwright, 2003). This article, about the need for accountability in MPs entitlements, referred to a New

South Wales Parliamentary Library research paper (Wilkinson, 2002) which detailed rises in MPs salaries, allowances and entitlements.

Two *Four Corners* TV programs have focused on problems with the Collins Class Submarine, which was the subject of a research paper, *Procuring Change: How Kockums was Selected for the Collins Class Submarine*, prepared by the Commonwealth Parliamentary Research Service (www.aph.gov.au/library/pubs/rp/2001-02/02rp04.pdf).

## Parliamentary papers

A parliamentary paper is a document which has been formally presented and tabled in a parliament. The reports of Royal Commissions, delegations and committees, annual reports of departments and agencies, white papers and Budget papers are usually presented to parliament.

Those parliamentary papers which are considered suitable for inclusion in the Commonwealth Parliamentary Papers Series are ordered to be printed, and copies of them are deposited in the National Library and in state libraries. They may also be available online.

Not all the documents presented to the Commonwealth parliament are ordered to be printed. Parliamentary papers which are tabled, but not printed, are not part of the Parliamentary Papers Series and may not be sent to the depository libraries. However, they are still public documents and they should be available for viewing by the public through the Table Office of the House of Representatives and the Senate, if they are not available online.

Australian state parliaments and the Legislative Assembly of the Northern Territory have also created Parliamentary Papers Series. Similar arrangements apply at state level to enable access to parliamentary papers.

Parliamentary papers generally attract qualified privilege. 'Fair and accurate' reports of their contents can be published with protection from the usual legal restrictions on reporting.

Commonwealth Parliamentary Papers are indexed in the Index to the Papers Presented to Parliament (www.aph.gov.au/house/pubs), which includes references to all tabled documents, not just parliamentary papers.

GovPubs: The Australian Government Publications Guide (www.nla.gov.au/govpubs) includes parliamentary papers. For New Zealand, look in Parliamentary Papers, New Zealand House of Representatives (www.clerk.parliament.govt.nz/Publications/ParliamentaryPapers).

## Reviews of administrative action

Reviews of administrative action are carried out by bodies such as the Administration Appeals Tribunal (www.aat.gov.au), the Commonwealth Ombudsman (www.comb.gov.au) and the Administration Review Council (www.ag.gov.au/www/arcHome.nsf/HeadingPagesDisplay/Publications?OpenDocument). Their reports document fraud, mismanagement and waste.

The Office of the Ombudsmen, New Zealand (www.ombudsmen.govt.nz) performs similar functions.

## Inquiries and commissions

As well as findings and recommendations, the reports of royal commissions such as the HIH Royal Commission (www.hihroyalcom.gov.au), commissions and committees of inquiry will include lists of the industry bodies, lobby groups or individuals who gave evidence or made submissions to the inquiry.

Inquiries and commissions investigating issues of current interest have the power to compel people to appear before them and answer questions, and people who have made submissions or given evidence may have still more evidence or information to supply to a researcher.

The reports of parliamentary select and standing committees are a mine of information. These committees are formed to investigate activities which are of public interest. Standing committees are established by the house for the life of parliament; joint standing committees include members from both houses of parliament. Select committees are appointed for a specific purpose.

Both Senate committees and House of Representatives committees have powers to summon witnesses to answer questions, and to call for papers to be written. They may ask for submissions from experts, organisations and any individual with an interest in the subject. Submissions made to these public forums are privileged; members and witnesses giving evidence are protected from being sued or prosecuted.

Each day's proceedings may be reported as news items. For instance, a front-page story, 'Navy Missed Doomed Boat', relies on testimony about navy patrols which was presented to a Senate committee investigating the sinking of the *Siev X* refugee boat (Stewart, 2002).

As well as immediate reports, over time the evidence presented can show up contradictions which will reward further investigation by a researcher. Staff working for parliamentary committees will send out copies of evidence as it is given, and transcripts and submissions should be available online or on request.

For the Parliament of Australia, details of inquiries are available from Committees (www.aph.gov.au/committee/committees_type.htm) and current inquiries by subject matter (www.aph.gov.au/committee/inquiries_subject.htm).

For New Zealand select committees, www.clerk. parliament.govt.nz/Programme/Committees sets out the NZ House of Representatives program.

## Senate estimates committees

Senate estimates committees are convened after the Budget each year to investigate the finances of government departments. At these hearings, members of the opposition get a chance to demand answers to tough questions from MPs and senior public servants. Their revelations often form the basis of significant news reports, such as 'A Conspiracy of Dunces' (Tingle, 2000) about the government's role in the downturn of its job agency Employment National.

You can find estimates hearings for the Parliament of Australia by selecting 'Guided Search' and 'Estimate Hearings for a Department' at parlinfoweb.aph.gov.au/piweb and transcripts by selecting 'Browse' and 'Committees'.

## Pecuniary interest registers

Pecuniary interest registers record what members of parliament and their families own or control, so that the public can see where there is a possible conflict of interest. For these registers, MPs should declare whether they or members of their family are directors or have a controlling interest in a company or trust, or own property.

Commonwealth government registers are available for perusal through the parliamentary clerk's office. Similar arrangements apply for state parliaments.

The Register of Ministers' Assets and Interests (www. dpmc. govt.nz/cabinet/cabinet/index.html) is held in the Cabinet Office, New Zealand Department of Prime Minister and Cabinet.

## EXERCISES

1   Find a copy of a commission or committee of inquiry report tabled in the Australian parliament in the last year and write a short 250-word story about an aspect of the report.

2   Using the findings and the list of the people who gave evidence and the submissions, research a story about the implementation of the recommendations of the inquiry.

### UNTANGLING THE POLITICAL TRAIL

To chase the political news, Elizabeth Meryment, Deputy Editor of *The Weekend Australian Review*, suggests keeping in mind that politics is about power, money and influence, and that political news usually involves changes in these areas.

Some of the actions that inspire political stories include the introduction of legislation that will affect peoples' lives, changes to the makeup of parties and movement on particular issues. Personality conflicts that have political significance are also newsworthy, as are events that could lead to changes in government.

As a political reporter, you will be constantly monitoring news reports as you keep in close touch with the premier's or prime minister's office to establish the government's agenda and its response to current issues and events. Other people to keep in close contact with are ministers and opposition spokespeople, their press secretaries and advisers, and the heads of government departments.

The most significant parliamentary events are

Question Time, the passage of legislation and debates about issues and new legislation, as well as the tabling of Budget papers and reports such as Royal Commissions and auditors' reports. Ministerial sources such as press secretaries and ministerial advisers may be prepared to brief you on the significance of a given change or event.

At times, officials and members of political parties will come to you with information, as will backbenchers and disgruntled former politicians.

When a story is already running and you need to get a reaction, depending on the issue, you could contact sources from industry officials, unionists, representatives of lobby groups, think tanks, organisations such as the Australian Medical Association or experts such as academics.

## GOVERNMENT DEPARTMENTS AND AGENCIES

The role of the public service bureaucracy is to implement the legislation which is issued by parliament. As they go about this task, government departments are accountable to the public for their actions, and they must account for the money they have spent. As a consequence, they are obliged to supply a great deal of information to the public.

Ministers are the political heads of departments, and they must be able to answer questions in parliament about who made the decisions, whether they were implemented, and how much it cost—making it necessary for departments to document who did what for whom, with how much taxpayers' money, and sometimes what went wrong.

Documents cover research reports, *Government Gazettes*, committee findings, inquiry reports, submissions, conference proceedings and so on. Government information may be in the form of books, journals, pamphlets, maps, kits, videos or microfilms.

Data from government documents provide the backbone of many articles, such as 'A Sick and Sorry Society' (Smith, 2000), which—as well as describing the problems caused by a shortage of mental health services—used government figures which showed that the state which spends the least on these services has the greatest need for them.

While the Commonwealth government in Canberra is the most prolific producer of Australian government information, state and local governments also document government activities—the policies, the decisions and the misdeeds.

*Statutory authorities* operate in a semi-independent manner. They are headed by a chairperson and are less strictly controlled than government departments, but they report to ministers and are expected to submit annual reports.

Some government bodies, such as the Queensland Investment Corporation, function as business enterprises or *Government Owned Corporations*. These enterprises trade and operate with commercial objectives, and may be listed on the Stock Exchange. Their activities are still subject to public sector accountability requirements, however.

## Using government documents

Governments generate an enormous number of documents, and the thickest, most dreary report may contain a page one story. While stories which are based on the findings of significant reports will appear immediately the document is

released, facts and figures drawn from government documents substantiate the claims made in stories which appear
long afterwards. *Sydney Morning Herald* reporter Malcolm
Brown says:

> I refer often to royal commission reports, which are avail-
> able in the *Herald* library. We also subscribe to a
> transcription service for royal commissions and commis-
> sions such as the NSW Police Integrity Commission,
> which is emailed to us and again is available internally
> through our electronic library access system. I make use
> of reports that are available on the internet. I wrote three
> chapters for my last book, *Australia's Worst Disasters*,
> largely from coroners' reports which were available on
> the internet. One was the Thredbo landslide of 1997,
> which I covered as a reporter. Another was the inquiry
> into the Sydney–Hobart race disaster, part of which I
> covered as a reporter. The third was the Blackhawk
> helicopter crash in Queensland, which I had had only
> passing contact with. I am writing another book, *Police
> Corruption*, based on the NSW Police Integrity Commis-
> sion inquiries of the last two years and am having
> transcripts of the hearings sent to me by the *Herald*
> library.

The first sign of a possible story could be an adverse
comment about an organisation in an Auditor-General's
report. A journalist could follow up by reading the annual
report for the organisation, then checking *Hansard* for any
statements in parliament on the subject before talking to the
staff of the relevant minister, and their counterpart in
the opposition.

*Canberra Times* Editor-in-Chief Jack Waterford suggests
(2002) that, to use government information successfully, you

need a fundamental understanding of how the relevant processes work—the structure of organisations, the relative powers of various officials and the way they make decisions. When you understand how a particular agency works, you will know who would have been involved in a process and when there has been a deviation from normal practice, and you can identify the people you should speak to.

Waterford recommends consulting the departments' rulebooks, policies and guidelines, as well as their annual reports and statements of the files the agencies hold. The records they keep will show what decisions were made and by whom, together with the reasons for those decisions. He says you need to read well beyond the executive summary of reports to find material which will produce stories that stand up.

## Which department or agency?

How do you know which department or agency is responsible for the issue you are investigating?

- *Commonwealth departments* administer legislation relevant to areas of broad national responsibility, such as defence, foreign affairs, immigration, overseas trade and higher education.
- *State* government departments administer public programs concerned with areas such as secondary and primary education, transport systems, police, hospitals and land-use planning.

There is overlap between the areas covered by different departments and agencies within the same sector, and between different levels of government. For instance, at the federal level there is a Department of Environment and

Heritage, while the responsibilities of departments at state level, such as the Victorian Department of Sustainability & Environment, also include the environment.

The range of activities of statutory authorities includes:

- communication—the Australian Broadcasting Corporation (www.abc.net.au);
- cultural—the Australian Film Commission (www.afc.gov.au);
- research—the Commonwealth Scientific and Industrial Research Organisation (CSIRO)(www.csiro.gov.au);
- education—the University of Sydney (www.usyd.edu.au);
- industry development—the Sugar Research and Development Corporation (www.srdc.gov.au).

Local government administrative responsibilities include land use, local roads, building permits and the provision of social, welfare and recreational services.

## Government directories

Use a directory such as one of the following to quickly get a breakdown of the functions of sections of government departments and agencies, and the names and telephone numbers of those with authority in these bodies.

- Australian Commonwealth Government departments and agencies: www.directory.gov.au;
- The Australian Government Directory: www.agd.com.au;
- Governments on the WWW, Australia: www.gksoft.com/govt/en/au.html.

Similar directories are produced for Australian state governments:

- Australian state and territory government departments: www.gov.au;
- *The New South Wales Government Directory*: www.directory.nsw.gov.au (and in print);
- *The Queensland Government Executive* Directory: www.qgd.qld.gov.au (and in print);
- *The Service SA Government Directory*: www.service.sa.gov.au/agencies.asp (and in print);
- *The Victorian Government Directory*: Government in Victoria: www.vic.gov.au (and in print);
- *The Western Australian Directory*: Online WA: www.onlinewa.com.au/standard/government (and in print);
- *The Tasmanian Government Directory*: http://directory.tas.gov.au (and in print);
- *The Australian Capital Territory Government Directory*: www.act.gov.au (and in print);
- *The Directory of Government in the Northern Territory*: www.nt.gov.au (and in print).

New Zealand government directories include:

- *The Directory of Official Information*, Ministry of Justice, New Zealand: www.justice.govt.nz/pubs/reports/1998/dir_off_info/index.html;
- Governments on the WWW, New Zealand: www.gksoft.com/govt/en/nz.html;
- govt.nz—New Zealand government departments and agencies: www.govt.nz/atoz;
- New Zealand central and local government services: www.govt.nz/services;
- *The New Zealand Government Directory* (Network Communications, Wellington, 1989– ).

Local government contacts are available through these directories:

- Australian federal, state, territory and local governments: www.gov.au;
- *The Australian Local Government Guide* (Information Australia Group, Melbourne, 1991– );
- Councils on the web (ALGA): www.alga.asn.au/ links/councils.php;
- New Zealand government departments and agencies: www.govt.nz/en/home;
- New Zealand central and local government services: www.govt.nz/services.

## Finding government information

You can find government information by navigating to the agencies through directories or portals, by researching in libraries, or by asking the agency directly for a copy of a report.

To find material linked from government sites using a search engine, restrict your search to the '.gov.au' domain. For instance, using Google, your search for material about 'recycling' would be: <recycling site:gov.au> or <recycling site:govt.nz>.

Depository libraries such as the National Library, state and university libraries hold copies of government publications, as the Library Deposit and Free Issues Scheme requires agencies to lodge copies of their publications with these libraries. Copies of local government documents may also be deposited in public libraries.

Library catalogues such as the National Library's catalogue (www.nla.gov.au/catalogue/index.html) list a wide range of government publications, while the National Library's *GovPubs: the Australian Government Publications Guide* (www. nla.gov.au/govpubs/about.html) explains their range.

## Government documents

This section explains and describes some categories of government publications which may assist journalists, writers, activists and documentary-makers in aspects of their research.

If you are looking for information about the activities of government departments and statutory authorities—for instance, the amount of money spent on consultants—look at the *annual reports* which government bodies are required to submit. Even the Governor-General has to do this (see www.gg.gov.au). As well as linking the agency to the relevant legislation, its annual return should include statements and statistical information about its goals, structure, finances and major activities.

Typical of the stories which jump out of annual reports is 'Complaints Against Police Pile Up' (Greber, 2000) which used information from a Criminal Justice annual report to highlight the rises in complaints of assaults made against police officers, and alleged police involvement in illicit drugs.

You can request copies of *birth, death and marriage certificates* through the links to state and territory offices included in Registrars of Births Deaths and Marriages (www.justice.qld.gov.au/bdm/home.htm), and through those in New Zealand Births, Deaths and Marriages (www.bdm.govt.nz/diawebsite.nsf/wpg_URL/Services-Births-Deaths-and-Marriages-Index?OpenDocument).

Information about government finances is available from the *Budget papers* and Budget-related papers series.

The Budget (www.budget.gov.au) is presented to the parliament by the Treasurer. The Treasury (www.treasury.gov.au) is responsible for economic trends and policy, while the Department of Finance (www.finance.gov.au) has an oversight function, and controls funds.

Budget papers include the Commonwealth Public Account, portfolio program estimates and Commonwealth's payments to other levels of government—states, the territories and local government authorities.

The Budget related papers report on government securities, national income and expenditure, income tax statistics, overseas aid and capital works, and social welfare programs.

Similar reports are published by the Australian states. The budgets and forecasts of the New Zealand government are available through the Treasury website (www.treasury.govt.nz/budgets).

When you are looking for people, one of the most useful aids can be the *Commonwealth electoral roll* which includes the names, addresses and occupations of voters. The roll is available in the head and regional offices of the Australian Electoral Commission (www.aec.gov.au).

The AEC also holds the maps of electorate boundaries, election statistics and political disclosures records (www. aec.gov.au/_content/how/political_disclosures/index.htm)—the lists of donations made to political parties or candidates standing for election. Stories about political party funding, such as 'Liberals Fail to Repay $4.5m "Shonky" Loan' (Martin, O'Loughlin & AAP, 1999), often use figures from the AEC returns.

Similar arrangements apply to state and local government elections with regard to election funding and donation information, which is also available through state Electoral Commissions, such as that in New South Wales (http://web.seo.nsw.gov.au/election_funding_nav/index.htm).

Elections New Zealand (www.elections.org.nz) includes similar information for New Zealand elections.

Under Australian federal and state laws, organisations and companies proposing to carry out a major building or mining project may be required to prepare a report about its probable effects. These *environmental impact statements* (EIS) such as the final EIS for Sydney's second airport proposal (www.dotars.gov.au/avnapt/sepb/eis/index.htm) may be made available for public examination through links on the organisation's website and by being placed in public libraries.

Disputes about environmental statements often make news, as in 'Channel Project Slammed' (Begg, 2004), a *Geelong Advertiser* story about concerns with proposed dredging projects.

Freedom of information legislation requires government bodies to make publicly available lists of the files they hold. Many departments place *indexed lists* online, such as the Department of Agriculture, Fisheries & Forestry (www.affa.gov.au/content/output.cfm?ObjectID=5A13A930-D311–4D77-BF004B6220FBD20D&contType=outputs).

Many government agencies invite external consultants to deliver some of their services on a contract basis. This outsourcing often motivates stories about such issues as ballooning costs and privacy problems—for example, 'Source of Angst' (Mitchell, 2000) in *The Australian*. Agencies also hire consultants on a contract basis to advise them, train their staff or perform other services.

To find out which contracts are being offered, use gazettes such as the *Commonwealth Purchasing and Disposal Gazette* (www.contracts.gov.au), portals such as Government Advertising (www.ads.gov.au), registers such as the Central Register of Major Government Contracts, Victoria (www.contracts.vic.gov.au/major/contracts.htm) or a list of agency contracts such as AFFA contracts (Department of Agriculture, Fisheries & Forestry) (www.affa.gov.au/content/output.cfm?ObjectID=D95401FE–027A–4594-A77413C7AE7E2DC7&contType=tools).

Governments publish *official gazettes* which notify other

agencies and the public about their decisions and actions of interest.

The weekly *Commonwealth of Australia Government Notices Gazette* (www.ag.gov.au/portal/govgazonline.nsf) contains a range of legislation, determinations, proclamations and department notices.

The *Public Service Gazette* (www.psgazetteonline.gov.au) includes notices about staff movements within the Australian Public Service.

Similar gazettes are issued by the state governments.

The *New Zealand Gazette* (www.dia.govt.nz/diaweb site.nsf/wpg_URL/Services-New-Zealand-Gazette-Index? OpenDocument) includes government and parliamentary notices, company notices, lists of bankruptcies and land transfer notices.

Government bodies also release copies of their *policy documents* (the rules and procedures by which a department makes decisions). Stories about inadequacies in nursing homes and the shortcomings of child-protection agencies may rely on establishing that the relevant agency's perform-ance is out of kilter with its policies, so finding the relevant policy will strengthen these stories.

Typical policy documents include aged care accredita-tion standards (www.accreditation.aust.com/accreditation/ standards.html), New South Wales State Environmental Planning Policies (SEPPs) (www.planning.nsw.gov.au/asp/ sepp.asp?where=sepp) and the New Zealand Oceans Policy (www.oceans.govt.nz). The Ministry of Agriculture and Forestry's MAF Policy portal (www.maf.govt.nz/mafnet/ profile/businesses/policy/index.html) is an index to policy.

Similar policies are formulated by state bodies, such as the Queensland State Purchasing Policy (www.qgm.qld. gov.au/policy2000/index.htm).

Government agencies employ researchers whose work

produces *research reports, papers* and *studies* which can provoke or strengthen stories, such as *Benchmarking Reconciliation and Human Rights* (www.hreoc.gov.au/social_justice/benchmarking/report.html) from the Human Rights and Equal Opportunity Commission, and *Deregulation of the NSW Dairy Industry* (www.agric.nsw.gov.au/reader).

Regular updates about urgent problems which could affect the public may be issued as bulletins, such as the *Australian Adverse Drug Reactions Bulletin*, from the Therapeutic Goods Administration (www.tga.gov.au/adr/aadrb.htm).

Research can also be compiled into collections such as *Environmental Sustainability Research* (www.fish.govt.nz/sustainability/research) from the New Zealand Ministry of Fishery.

The accountability requirement which applies to government organisations means they are open to *reviews and audits* including the scrutiny of the Auditor-General whose role it is to uncover and document mismanagement and bureaucratic waste.

Auditor-General reports are a popular source of news, such as '$630m Splurged on Consultants' (McKinnon, 2000), a front page *Courier-Mail* story.

Other bodies which scrutinise government processes, activities and decisions include the Australian National Audit Office, which publishes the ANAO Audit Reports (www.anao.gov.au), the Administrative Appeals Tribunal, the various Ombudsmen and the Administrative Review Council.

If you need to find *international government information*, portals such as Worldwide Governments on the WWW (www.gksoft.com/govt/en/world.html) and the National Library's European government internet resources (www.nla.gov.au/gov/eu.html) can help you.

Print publications such as *The Far East and Australasia* (Europa Publications, London) include regional surveys, organisations and statistics.

A daunting amount of detailed documentation emerges each day from the United Nations (www.un.org/english/index.shtml). Use the UN Documentation Centre (www.un.org/documents) as a guide to its resolutions, records and publications.

European resources include UK Online (www.open.gov.uk) and Europa—The European Union On-Line (www.europa.eu.int), which contains press releases, statistics, publications and databases.

The US Government Printing Office produces GPO Access (www.gpoaccess.gov), a service which distributes official information from all three levels of government, or use the US Government portal, FirstGov (www.firstgov.gov) and the GrayLIT Network (http://graylit.osti.gov) to find US technical reports.

## EXERCISE

Pick a current issue and find a government report or document from the categories above which is relevant to this topic. Write a story using the documents you have found.

## UNCOVERING SOCIAL HISTORY

### Siobhan McHugh

My first research tip is not to ignore what appear to be tangents you uncover, as they often end up becoming the main story.

*Minefields and Miniskirts* (McHugh, 1993) started out as a commission to write the history of Australian nurses in Vietnam, but it became clear from the first two interviews that women spoke differently about war and its effects than men. I followed this perception up by interviewing women of all kinds who had been in Vietnam during the war—entertainers, journalists, secretaries and diplomats, as well as medical and humanitarian workers—and got a far richer, more complex book.

Likewise, *Cottoning On* (McHugh, 1996) was supposed to be a history of how the cotton industry grew out of surplus irrigation water in the 1960s, and a study of its now-controversial use of water. But everyone I spoke to in the cotton industry—growers, residents and greenies—raised the issue of chemical use as well. Once I started investigating pesticide use, the abysmal regulation of aerial spraying and the perceived health effects of these chemicals on the communities, I knew I could not write a history of cotton-growing without addressing this issue.

It was very difficult to research, being highly technical, officially sensitive and hard to prove. I took an extra year to write the book, about half of which is an investigation into the use of chemicals in the industry. That research saw me shortlisted for both a Premier's History Award and a Eureka Science prize. And (perhaps by total coincidence) the Environmental Protection Agency changed the laws on aerial spraying soon after my book came out.

Second, rather than seeking evidence to back up your preconceived idea, keep an open mind and be prepared to change it if what you discover warrants it.

Also, don't put people in boxes, on one 'side' or the other. 'Goodies' will always have negative qualities, while 'baddies' are never all bad. This applies to virtually every interview of the hundreds I've done. When you like someone, you are tempted to gloss over their inadequacies or misjudgements, and present their positive attributes without referring to their flaws. Equally, when you know someone holds an unpalatable view, such as a racist attitude, it's easy to 'bag' that person.

Writing is as much about what you withhold as what you say. Clearly, you should not misrepresent, but you also do your interviewees—and your readers—a disservice if you do not paint a fully rounded picture, however much it gets in the way of a neat, linear argument.

Third, note sources for all relevant quotes, statistics and so on at the time you read them, as six months from now you will never remember where they came from.

Fourth, be persistent. While writing *The Snowy* (McHugh, 1989) it took me six months to gain access to the inquests into 112 fatalities on the Snowy Mountains Hydro-Electric Scheme. Access was at first refused by the Attorney-General on privacy grounds, which I successfully appealed against, citing prior descriptions in newspaper reports at the time. Then, the inquests were physically hard to track down: some had been archived, but the rest were stored higgledy-piggledy in courtrooms around the state. When they were finally transferred to government archives for me to view, I could only see about two or three boxes at a time, then had to queue up again at the end of a long line of amateur genealogists keen to engage the counter staff in discussion about their forebears. It took me weeks to get through them all—but it enabled me to make strong statements in *The Snowy* about safety, accidents and attitudes on the construction, a chapter singled out by one critic as being particularly powerful.

Fifth, do your homework! Being prepared enables you to get much more from an interview, at both a human and a research level.

One of my final interviews for *Cottoning On* was with the environmental director of the Australian Cotton Foundation (ACF), the growers' body. I hadn't left it until last by accident. For two years I had been accumulating evidence about the use of toxic chemicals in the industry, and his would be the official response. I had heard from residents in cotton country how impenetrably scientific (to them) his answers were. They could not contest what he said because they didn't have the technical knowledge to hand. I was determined I would be different.

I went back over all my research as assiduously as if I was swotting for an exam. I had, in another life, obtained a Bachelor of Science, so I wasn't afraid of the lingo. But the volume of data was huge, and I knew I had to retain it mentally in order to pick up instantly on any interesting revelations he made.

The day came and I asked him about a well-documented incident near Moree in 1991 (now recorded in the book). A team of cotton chippers was hoeing weeds when a plane started spraying in an adjacent field. Soon a chipper smelt something like 'flyspray' and her eyes began to sting. The chemical from the plane evidently was being blown onto them by the wind. The foreman had the news radioed to the pilot and asked him to stop, but he didn't. Some of the workers took refuge in a minibus.

By the next morning, most of the chippers had experienced headaches, sore eyes and throats, and coughs—symptoms consistent with having been exposed to endosulfan, the active ingredient in the spray. A government

Agricultural Health Unit, which fortuitously was in the area, examined sixteen workers and filed a report.

The case went to court—but, despite the magistrate observing that there was no doubt that the pilot had 'deliberately sprayed pesticide' onto fields adjacent to where he was aware the chippers were working, the pilot walked away scot-free. This was because the woefully inept legislation required the workers to prove that through that spraying, he had 'wilfully . . . caused a risk of injury by a pesticide'.

Nonetheless, the case was embarrassing for the industry. At first, the ACF spokesman tried to play it down, stating that 'none of those people, until the symptoms were described to them, exhibited any symptoms'. In fact, as I knew from reading her report, Dr Lyn Clarke of Aghealth took pains to point out that the chippers were interviewed in such a way as to eliminate any form of auto-suggestion. Warning one: I was getting misinformation.

The spokesman then said that the pesticide used was 'a cholinesterase inhibitor'. (Cholinesterase is an enzyme, the blood level of which, after an event, can indicate exposure to certain chemicals.) 'When they tested those people,' he went on, 'there was no depression of cholinesterase . . . now that is a direct link of exposure. That is one of the reasons the case was dismissed.'

From my reading, I knew two things. First, the chemical in question, endosulfan, is an organochlorine— a compound that does not respond to cholinesterase. So to imply that the lack of depression of cholinesterase meant there had been no exposure to endosulfan was nonsense. Cholinesterase worked on totally different pesticides, such as organophosphates.

Second, this was not a ground on which the case had

been dismissed; that was on the interpretation of the word 'wilfully'. I had read the magistrate's report.

I gave him my most guileless look and asked: 'But isn't endosulfan an organochlorine? In which case, as we know (I said it as if we were Watson and Crick, communing as equals on our discovery), it wouldn't respond to cholinesterase.'

Over the next 90 minutes, I grilled him on every worrisome aspect of cotton and chemicals I had gathered or observed over the past year. Later, he observed to someone who reported it back to me, that I was one of the rudest people who'd ever interviewed him.

The tape resides in the Mitchell Library at the State Library of New South Wales, and I don't think it will show that I was rude. I was, however, persistent, informed and looking for straight answers. I would never have got them had it not been for my exhaustive research. My parents would have been pleased to know that my science training—never formally used until then—came in handy at last.

## LAND TITLES

Property searches can tell you what land or property people own, or have owned, often how much they bought and sold it for, who they own the land with and whether they have a mortgage over it. Most land title information is publicly available so that anyone wanting to buy land or property can be sure of its ownership.

This information often underpins business stories, profiles and biographies and investigative reports. It can also produce some great celebrity gossip. When James Packer (son of Australia's most powerful media proprietor) split with actor Kate Fischer in 1998, reporters could say the title for their Bondi Beach property had been transferred to her name by checking the land title register for New South Wales.

Researchers such as documentary-makers and family historians can use land title information to find out who owned a piece of land a hundred years ago.

## Finding land title information

State government departments hold records of land ownership, and provide this information to the public. A fee is usually payable for this. You can search in person at the Land Title Office, or by mail, fax or online. Professional land title searchers such as Ayres Britton can also be hired for a fee.

At times, you may also need to consult other government bodies which have responsibilities in land management, including planning, managing Crown lands and seabed and riverbed leases.

To begin your search for land title information, a crucial piece of data is the land's identifying number, usually the lot/plan number. The volume and folio number or the title reference number may also be used. This number is available through local councils and stated on rate notices. Or, if this number is not available, you can begin with the street address.

You can hire an information broker to obtain the information for you, in return for a higher fee. Information brokers such as CITEC Confirm (www.confirm.com.au) and Lawpoint (www.lawpoint.com.au) are businesses which buy and sell information—they pay agencies for access to their information, and then sell this data to the public for a fee.

## Information supplied by title searches

Although land title searching is similar across the Australian states and in New Zealand, the kind of information provided varies. It may include:

- the title—the current registered proprietors, encumbrances and caveats;
- historical information—dealings on a title, changes to the proprietor;
- survey plans of subdivisions;
- a name search—list of current titles held under a name;
- community title schemes;
- a vendor statement—last sales details for an address;
- crown leases; and
- imaged plans.

## Land Title Offices

At the *New South Wales* Land and Property Information Office, you can begin searching with the land description or the portion in parish, the location of a piece of land, a street address, or a proprietor's name.

The land and property description shown on council rate notices will show the folio identifier (title reference) of the title you want to search. The folio identifier corresponds to the lot and DP (deposited plan) number on the property description. A Mapping Index is available when the land description is not known; title details can be supplied for a street address.

More information is available from *A Guide to Searching New South Wales Land Title Records* (www.lands.nsw.gov.au) and *Land and Property Information Searches New South Wales* (http://lpi-online.lpi.nsw.gov.au) from the New South Wales Department of Information Technology and Management.

Information brokers can be contacted through Land and Property Searches New South Wales—Information Brokers (http://lpi online.lpi.nsw.gov.au/lpsearch/brokers.html).

At the *Victoria* Land Information Centre, you can do a Land Index Search if the volume folio identifier is unknown. Property identification details are available online through their interactive map to locate a lot on plan number.

More information is available from Land Victoria—Titles and Property Certificate Service (www.land.vic.gov.au).

Information brokers can be contacted through Land Channel: Land Victoria: Brokers and Data Service Providers (www.land.vic.gov.au).

*Queensland* land title information is available through the Department of Natural Resources and Mines' Land Titles (www.nrm.qld.gov.au/property/titles/index.html).

Information brokers can be contacted through External Distributors (www.nrm.qld.gov.au/products/distributors.php?type=Real-time+Online).

Land Title information in *South Australia* is provided through the Land Services Group's LOTS (Land Ownership and Tenure System). To search the system, you need the certificate of title reference, owner details or the address details.

More information is available from the Department of Administrative and Information Services (www.landservices.sa.gov.au and www.dias.gov.au).

Information about *Western Australian* land title data is provided through the Land Enquiry Centre, with instructions available at Department of Land Information (www.dola.wa.gov.au).

At the *Tasmanian* Land Data Registration Branch, the most reliable access to the title information held within the LIST Land Information System is via the volume and folio number for the land parcel. More information is available from The LIST Land Information System Tasmania (www.thelist.tas.gov.au).

At the *Northern Territory* Land Titles Office, title information can be accessed by lot number and location, owner's name, or the volume and folio reference of the certificate of title. More information is available from the Northern Territory Department of Justice (www.nt.gov.au/justice/graphpages/contacts/landtitle.shtml).

Information about titles in the *Australian Capital Territory* is available from Land Title Forms (www.canberra connect.act.gov.au/landplanningbuild/buysellproperty/landtitleforms.html).

To search the records at Land Information *New Zealand* you will need the land district your search relates to, the appropriate record reference number and the record type. More information is available from Landonline New Zealand (www.landonline.govt.nz) and Researchers and Historians (LINZ) (www.linz.govt.nz/rcs/linz/pub/web/root/audiences/researchersandhistorian/index.jsp).

## LOCAL GOVERNMENT

The functions of local government include the construction and maintenance of local roads and bridges, libraries, social welfare such as home help and child-care centres, and recreational services. Its powers are held by delegation from, and under the supervision of, state governments.

Council municipalities may be divided into electoral districts or wards, each of which elects one councillor to represent them for a term, often three years. In each council committees of councillors or aldermen are elected to manage their responsibilities, with a mayor acting as the public spokesperson and the ceremonial head of council.

Local government is a great source of stories because

council decisions often affect people in an immediate and very direct way. For example, in flood-prone Brisbane, the revelation that a study, which had not been publicised, had forecast that the next major flood could be up to 2 metres higher than allowed for in the town plan produced a series of major stories (Hedley, 2003).

## Local government responsibilities

This level of government provides services such as waste removal, and community resources such as libraries, swimming pools and other recreational facilities. Local government staff may construct roads, carry out health inspections and license pets.

Local government is also usually responsible for processing building approvals and land use applications. The documents related to land use which should be available from council offices include proposals to resume land, successful and unsuccessful development applications, decisions on appeals, a rateable land register and lists of ratepayers.

A list of submissions, or the actual submissions, made by organisations and individuals in response to development applications are usually available at the council's offices for viewing by the public, or they may be accessible via council's website. Plans for major developments are often placed in public libraries.

The general meetings and agendas of councils will usually be open to the public. Committee meetings are often open, but they may be closed when particular matters are discussed. The minutes of meetings and documents used in meetings should be available afterwards from their website, such as those for the Brisbane City Council (www.brisbane.qld.gov.au and search on 'minutes') or through council offices or public libraries.

## Local government documents

Documents relating to the internal operations of council should also be available, such as their annual reports, auditors' reports, strategic plans, delegations (Council officers who have decision-making powers), financial reports, register of policy documents, tender documents, salary packages for senior staff and councillors' expenses and payments policy.

The elected members, who may be called councillors or aldermen, usually work part-time and therefore tend to carry other responsibilities as well as their council duties. As with other politicians, the public has a right to access pecuniary interest details such as councillors' employment, business partnerships, and contracts between the councillor (or their business) and the council. Details about candidates' election campaign donations should also be provided.

The *Local Government Acts* for each state, including the laws about disclosure of interests, are available through Austlii (www.austlii.edu.au), the Australasian Legal Information Institute legislation database.

## Local government guides

To find data about council area populations and boundaries, as well as their employees, mayors, wards and major projects, use guides such as the *Australian Local Government Guide* (Information Australia, Melbourne) or *The Australian Local Government Yearbook* (North Hargreen Publishing Company, Melbourne).

You can obtain contact information for local governments through directories such as www.gov.au, The Australian Local Government Association (www.alga.asn.au) and find out about local and regional government in New Zealand (www.govt.nz).

Journals such as local government bulletins can be a good place to pick up background information about current local government issues.

Local interest groups, local businesses, business associations and residents' action groups will also often have information about council activities.

## EXERCISE

Attend a meeting of your local council or find the agenda, minutes and report from a recent meeting. Contact at least one of the people involved, get a comment from them and write an eight-par news report about a current issue or proposal discussed at the meeting.

## FREEDOM OF INFORMATION

There are many beliefs about freedom of information (FOI). One is that FOI makes government open and transparent. However, others say that governments are increasingly using exemptions to limit access to sensitive material.

Some journalists are using FOI requests, including Pilita Clark (2003) who says: 'I have made a number of Freedom of Information applications, with some successful results and I would encourage all new journalists to use this tool aggressively and imaginatively.'

In practice, there are many ways of using FOI, and you may not, in fact, need it at all.

### FOI legislation

FOI was intended to give the public a legal right to access government documents. The Commonwealth of Australia passed the first *Freedom of Information Act* in 1982, and during the two decades since then the states and some territories have passed their own FOI legislation.

Information can be requested from agencies such as government departments and authorities, government ministers and regulatory bodies. Statutory authorities like universities, public hospitals, state boards and commissions can also be required to provide their records.

## FOI for individuals

Using the FOI legislation, individuals may ask to see or correct documents about themselves, such as their government employment records. This is the most common use of the legislation, and is usually successful.

## Publicly available material

For some other situations, though, FOI may not be necessary. Members of groups such as lobbyists and unions may make FOI requests to find information about the routine decisions of government, such as zoning decisions or customs determinations.

However, *Canberra Times* Editor-in-Chief Jack Waterford (1999b) says this kind of information is often available without needing to use FOI. He recommends that anyone wanting this information should first try to find it using publicly available sources such as government directories.

## Exempt documents

Journalists and activists may ask to see material which may cause problems for government, but these FOI requests are not always successful.

A broad range of exemptions can be used to block access to government material. Documents which are exempt from release under FOI include those brought before cabinet or executive council; or those which relate to investigations by external bodies, law enforcement or public safety; or those which contain information which affects the economy, legal proceedings, personal or business affairs. These exemptions are blamed by many researchers for the poor record of success in obtaining access to sensitive documents.

However, Waterford says that, as well as the exemptions, and FOI taking too long for the deadlines of many journalists, part of the reason for the lack of successful requests for sensitive material is that journalists do not have enough detailed knowledge of the processes of government to follow the 'paper trail' successfully.

He says the more that journalists effectively exploit other publicly available resources to obtain information, the less they will need to use FOI.

## Precise applications

Departments publish statements about who they are, what they do, their boards, powers and functions, and the working files and documents they hold. Reading these, together with the internal rules, guidelines, standards and manuals officers use to do their jobs, can establish how decisions should have been made.

Industrious researchers who use these guides may be able to go straight to the appropriate person or division and obtain the information immediately. Or, armed with this knowledge and with the help of the FOI officers whose role includes helping members of the public to frame their requests, they can prepare a focused, precise submission which will have more chance of success.

Journalist Bob Burton files stories for the *British Medical*

*Journal*, the Bangkok office of Inter-Press, and edits *Disinfo-pedia* for the US-based non-profit media group, the Center for Media and Democracy. With a long record of using FOI successfully, he stresses (2004) the advantages of making and using contacts:

> Using FOI to go fishing for documents is possible but potentially expensive and very time consuming. Far better to know what document or file you are after at the outset. While most public servants are very wary about leaking documents they are equally often happy to confirm the existence of a document or even the file number to help facilitate you exercising your rights under FOI legislation. So staying in touch with your departmental contacts can help you zero in on what you are interested in and save you time and costs.

In those cases where FOI requests are successful, the documents obtained will usually underpin only part of any story that results. Ricketson and Snell (2002) point out that 'genuinely important news stories about government are rarely simple', and suggest that the use of FOI is likely to add another piece to the jigsaw about incompetent decision-making or to build pressure against a government, rather than being the whole story.

## FOI requests

To make an FOI request, ring the FOI contact officer of the relevant department and clarify whether that agency holds the types of documents you need. Then write to the FOI officer, asking for information under the relevant FOI legislation. Expect your request to take some weeks to be filled. Explain precisely the kind of documents you need, the projects you are interested in, when they would have been created and the section or person who was likely to have been involved.

Enclose whatever payment is appropriate. The usual cost to apply to an Australian Commonwealth agency for non-personal affairs information is A$30. There may be extra charges for processing and copying. Justify briefly why it is in the public interest for this information to be released; the fees may be waived for requests to federal government departments if granting of access is seen to be in the public interest.

If your request is refused, you can ask the original agency to review its decision, and then appeal its decision to the Administrative Appeals Tribunal (AAT). A range of fees can be charged for internal and external reviews.

## FOI offices

There are FOI offices for all levels of government. Commonwealth and state offices with key FOI instructions are listed below:
- Commonwealth Attorney-General's Department: www.ag. gov.au/foi;
- Department of Justice and Attorney-General, Queensland: www.justice.qld.gov.au/dept/foi.htm;
- Office of the Information Commissioner, Western Australia: www.foi.wa.gov.au;
- Attorney-General's Department, New South Wales: www.lawlink.nsw.gov.au/crd.nsf/pages/foiindex;
- Department of Justice, Victoria: www.foi.vic.gov.au;
- State Records of South Australia: www.archives.sa.gov. au/services/public;
- Chief Minister's Department, Australian Capital Territory: www.cmd.act.gov.au;

- Department of Justice and Industrial Relations, Tasmania: www.justice.tas.gov.au/justice/info_foi.htm;
- Department of Justice, Northern Territory: www.nt.gov.au/justice;
- The Office of the Privacy Commissioner of New Zealand: www.knowledge-basket.co.nz/privacy/top.html.

International sites with FOI information include freedominfo.org (www.freedominfo.org) for FOI laws around the world, and FOI Sites on the Internet (www.law.utas.edu.au/foi/bookmarks/FOI_index.html) from the FOI Research Unit, University of Tasmania.

# 6

# FINDING OLD SCENTS AND NEW TRAILS

## PUBLIC RELATIONS AND PRESS RELEASES

Public relations (PR), press secretaries, community relations, public affairs, corporate communications, media liaison—whatever it's called, these professionals work to create favourable relationships with bodies and people significant to their clients, including journalists.

While many PR firms and operators operate in an ethical manner, it is important to remember that they exist to promote the interests of their clients. They try to shape opinion, manage issues and get media coverage for their products by supplying information which presents their organisation, issue or event in the best possible light.

They may present only a selective version of events, slanted to suit their client's agenda. To see this expert 'spin' in action, browse through the 'Spin of the week' case studies collected in PR Watch (www.prwatch.com). They may make it hard to speak to people within the organisation, to ensure that researchers speak only to sources who will say things which are favourable to their client.

The good thing about PR people is that they are happy to do some of the legwork for you. For example, if you want some background about extensions to a major public institution, the Public Relations department will be generous with information about the development's history and progress. They will supply statistics, photographs, maps, diagrams and in-house publications on request. Without even being asked, they may also send you videos of news-worthy events, other graphics and audio interviews.

However, they will usually only supply material which presents their organisation favourably. Other relevant data about cost overruns and corruption in the tendering process is unlikely to be included in their attractive information pack.

All of the above applies even if the PR agency is attached to a source which is usually seen as reputable, such as a government department or university. The source—the department or university—may be credible, meaning that you can quote them, but you still should not accept uncrit-ically the claims they make in their media releases.

However, it can be a mistake to ignore media releases. In order to satisfy their requirement to put information on the record, government departments may bury bad or damaging news in the second last paragraph of a long press release (Castle, 2003).

It can also be unwise to dismiss press releases which are sloppily or incoherently written. A release from an environ-mental organisation may be badly written by a volunteer, but it may contain vital intelligence. To check it out, contact the person or organisation and ask them for documents or evidence to justify their claims.

However, beware of pseudo-activist front organisations, such as environmental groups set up by PR firms (Stauber & Rampton, 1995).

## Your own agenda

It is always wise to find your own sources rather than relying on press secretaries and media minders, and to set your own agenda rather than accepting the view of issues or events presented in press releases and at press conferences.

## News conferences

News conferences are often organised with the aim of controlling the information given out; there is always some level of manipulation.

As well as attending and asking questions at news conferences, try to make the occasion more valuable for you by using the event as a point of contact to develop your own story, by setting up a one-on-one interview afterwards (Castle, 2003).

Although press releases and news conferences can help you to find a story, they offer only a starting point. It is vital to research your own story from your own angle, getting your own quotes, comments and reactions.

## Using press releases

Use media releases as an alerting tool, to let you know that an event is to happen or that a meeting will take place. You may be able to take some information from them, but their contents need to be checked and any claims they make need to be confirmed with sources elsewhere.

A crucial difference between press releases and stories which have been published in newspapers, magazines and newsletters, newswire stories and transcripts of broadcasts—all of which are copyright—is that you can quote from press releases, particularly facts such as 'A spokesperson for the Minister said today the North Point bridge would cost taxpayers $30 million'.

Check out the latest releases or sign up to receive press releases by email from AAP MediaNet Media Releases (www.aapmedianet.com.au).

## Archives and transcripts

Archives of press releases and the transcripts of news conferences can be a rich source of valuable information. The searchable archives provided by government departments are a record of their official promises, which can later be matched against how well those promises were kept.

For example, if you want to look for the government statements about topics such as people in refugee camps, you can search government media releases by portfolio through the Commonwealth of Australia media releases (http://media.fed.gov.au).

Pick up New Zealand parliamentary press conference transcripts from New Zealand Post Cabinet Press Conference Transcripts (www.beehive.govt.nz/transcripts.cfm) or releases from a variety of agencies through Scoop New Zealand News (www.scoop.co.nz/mason/).

Press releases from Australian business, government and community organisations are available from the Press Release Centre (www.pressrelease.com.au), while those from Australian universities are linked through the Australian Vice-Chancellors' Committee (www.avcc.edu.au). See also clearly explained.com/news/unipress_au.html.

## EXERCISE

Find a press release from a government department, a company or organisation on the same topic as a current major news story, and compare it with the news reports, looking for similarities and differences. Has the story been reported with the same spin as the press release? To what degree has the story been developed beyond the press release?

## NEWS REPORTS

Reading a number of newspapers and listening to or watching broadcasts is a basic bedrock research tool for finding current news, quick facts, and upcoming events.

Journalist Anne Lim, who writes for *The Australian*, says she checks all the main Australian papers each day as a matter of course.

As well as the news reports, scanning other sections of newspapers, such as the 'Letters to the editor' and the opinion pages, will help to keep you informed about public opinion changes. Opinion pieces are written by experts or senior journalists and contain different points of view about current topics.

### Copyright restrictions

Almost everything which has been published or broadcast is copyright, either to the author or to the publication in which it appears. This means that you cannot copy any part of it without asking permission of the copyright holder. Any references you make to copyright material should be minor and contain a clear attribution to the published report: 'In a report on ABC News Radio yesterday, the Premier promised to hold an election within six months'.

### Finding articles and transcripts

You can find articles and transcripts online through the various publications' websites. Major Australian sites include the Fairfax f2 network site (www.f2.com.au) for publications such as the *Sydney Morning Herald*, *The Age*, *Business Review Weekly* and Fairfax community newspapers.

For any articles from News Limited's national, state, regional and local newspapers, including *The Australian*, go to its website News.com.au portal (www.news.com.au).

If you want to check what was said on air, the transcripts of radio and television broadcasts may be available through the broadcaster, such as ABC News Online (www.abc.net. au/news). The ABC Radio National website (www.abc. net.au/rn) contains transcripts and recordings of its programs, while the subscription-based Radio New Zealand Transcripts Database (www.knowledge-basket.co.nz/rnz) contains transcripts of broadcasts since 1998.

Major New Zealand sites include the *New Zealand Herald* (www.nzherald.co.nz) and Radio New Zealand (www. radionz.co.nz), which provides audio files of its programs. The Fairfax New Zealand site, Stuff: NZ Newspapers (www.stuff.co.nz/nz_newspapers.html) includes New Zealand newspapers and regional news.

Most major newspapers provide free access to a selection of articles published that day or in the last week or so, while there is usually a charge to retrieve articles from their archives.

## Archives

Newspaper archives usually contain most, though not all, of the articles which appeared in the newspaper. Some archives contain the entire laid-out publication as a pdf file. If you are researching funding cuts to public broadcasters, for instance, you could search a newspaper archive using keywords such as 'ABC funding cuts' to find articles which contain these words.

Search the archive of Fairfax publications at News Store (http://newsstore.f2.com.au/apps/newsSearch.ac), or the News Limited publications archive at News Text (www. newstext.com.au).

Archive services such as New Zealand Newztext (www.knowledge-basket.co.nz/kete/whereis.html) collect the contents of many newspapers.

Charges for finding and retrieving articles are usually by unit or by time. Charging by unit means paying for each article you find and retrieve, often at a cost of around A$2 an article; charging by time means paying for a day, a month or a year's access to the archive, as with the *Financial Times*' World Press Monitor Service (http://news.ft.com/FTCorporate/Site/html/uk/ft/world_press.html).

International news sites which include archives include ABYZ News Links (www.abyznewslinks.com), a portal with links to sources listed under geographical regions. BBC News (http://news.bbc.co.uk) includes worldwide news reports and country profiles. Stories from the UK *Guardian* and *Observer* newspapers can be freely retrieved through the Guardian Unlimited archive (www.guardian.co.uk/Archive).

Articles can also be found and searched using services such as LexisNexis and Factiva. (See the section on 'Finding articles in indexes and databases' later in this chapter.)

**News compilations**

If you're looking for background about big news events, news compilations which are collections of stories about current issues can make the task easier. See the *Sydney Morning Herald* News Specials (www.smh.com.au/specials) for some examples.

**News directories and portals**

Newspapers are listed under states and titles at Australian Newspapers Online (www.nla.gov.au/npapers), a National Library site.

International portals which list newspapers under regions and countries include NewsLink (www.newslink.org), the International News Archives on the Web (www.ibiblio.org/

slanews/internet/intarchives.htm), The Internet Public Library—
Newspapers (www.ipl.org/div/news) and Onlinenewspapers.
com (www.onlinenewspapers.com).

## Newswire services

Newswire services such as Australian Associated Press
(AAP) (www.aap.com.au) employ journalists who file news
stories and photographs which are sold to government,
corporate or media organisations, including portals such
as Yahoo!. These services buy the right to run newswire
articles and graphics, which will then appear in their publications or on their websites. These stories are updated
frequently, and breaking news often shows up first on a
newswire.

Scoop—New Zealand news (www.scoop.co.nz/mason/)
links to New Zealand newswires, while Yahoo! News
(http://dailynews.yahoo.com) collects newswire stories
under topics and regions.

Well-known international newswire services include
Agence France-Presse (www.afp.com), Reuters (www.reuters.
com) and The Associated Press (www.ap.org). UN Wire (www.
unfoundation.org/unwire) is a news briefing about the
United Nations and global affairs which includes a searchable archive.

IPS Inter Press Service: The Global Gateway
(www.ips.org) specialises in global issues, while the independent media centre Indymedia (www.indymedia.org) allows
independent observers to post their stories and opinions.

## Alerting services

Alerting services such as BriefMe.com (www.Briefme.com)
will monitor and clip articles for you if you choose a subject

or supply key words to the service. You will then receive the most recent stories about your chosen topic by email. These personalised news services are useful for researchers working on long-term projects.

## Headline aggregators

Headline aggregators such as Google News (www.news.google.com), Yahoo! News (http://dailynews.yahoo.com) and NewsNow (www.newsnow.co.uk) prepare a list of headlines from breaking stories taken from newspapers, newswires and broadcast outlets.

Services such as 1stHeadlines (www.1stheadlines.com), The WorldNews Network (www.wnnetwork.com) and News is Free (www.newsisfree.com) group headlines under topics such as health, entertainment, politics, sport, etc., or by geographic area.

## News search engines

Specialised search engines such as Google News (www.news.google.com) and Yahoo! Directory News and Media (http://dir.yahoo.com/news) allow you to restrict your search to news stories and graphics. Use a news search engine such as these if you have a specific term to look for, such as 'anthrax inoculation'.

You can restrict your search by country or category using News Trawler (www.newstrawler.com) or choose current news stories from the past five days using RocketNews (www.rocketnews.com).

## Printed newspapers

You can access printed newspapers in libraries, particularly public and academic libraries. Public libraries will hold a selection of local, interstate and sometimes overseas newspapers; they may also hold back-copies for three months. State and other libraries also hold overseas newspapers in a variety of formats.

The National Library of Australia holds all the capital city dailies, as well as country newspapers, newspapers published by ethnic groups and political organisations, and newspapers representing special interests.

For researchers such as family historians, state libraries and major public libraries hold collections of newspapers going back decades, or even centuries. In some cases, state libraries will hold newspapers in the original paper format, or on microfilms (in reduced size on reels), microfiche (transparent cards), or microprint (opaque white cards).

Universities usually subscribe to a range of newspapers relevant to their teaching areas. For instance, Griffith University libraries in Brisbane hold the major metropolitan, local, national and capital city newspapers, selected suburban papers, a range of foreign-language Australian ethnic newspapers and international newspapers including at least one major British, Northern American, European and Asian daily newspaper.

To find newspapers in libraries, look in the library catalogue under the title of the newspaper (e.g., *The Age*).

## EXERCISE

Find a recent article from a major newspaper, a newswire and one overseas newspaper about a recent major environmental, health or legal issue.

## PERIODICALS: MAGAZINES, NEWSLETTERS AND JOURNALS

You might know the latest news, but what does it really mean? As well as it being fun to browse through features in magazines, reading longer articles helps you to understand the background to current events and the people who make things happen.

Longer articles and broadcast programs provide stimulating new perspectives about significant people and institutions, not to mention great graphics and even giveaways.

Researchers looking into an industry or profession need to read periodicals in the area because new developments such as medical breakthroughs and problems with products will often show up first in these publications.

Articles in magazines could be written by journalists, submitted by keen amateurs or commissioned from experts, so their reliability as an information source varies.

## Popular magazines

Articles in popular magazines such as *The Bulletin* (http://bulletin.ninemsn.com.au) and the *New Zealand Women's Weekly* (www.wilsonandhorton.co.nz/wh_companies/ magazines_and_books/nz_womens_weekly) are usually written by journalists, so they are easy to understand and a good way to inform yourself about a new topic. However, the quality of the information in these publications can vary. Some articles are based on solid research but since the sources used by the writer will not always be shown, they may not be a reliable resource.

Your local public library will hold a selection of popular magazines and keep back-copies for at least a few months. Check the title of the magazine in the library's catalogue.

Most popular magazines will have a website, although often only a few of their articles are linked from their site. Find popular magazines online with portals such as Yahoo! Magazines (http://dir.yahoo.com/News_and_Media/Magazines) and New Zealand Top Media (www.business.

vu.edu.au/bho2250/Top20Media/TopmediaNZ.htm).

E-zines, or electronic magazines, can be found through portals such as (http://directory.google.com/Top/News/ Magazines_and_E-zines/E-zines).

## Specialised magazines and journals

There's a magazine for almost every interest, such as the futurist *21C* (www.21cmagazine.com), the consumer magazine *Choice* (www.choice.com.au), *The Economist* (www.economist.com), *Art News* (www.artnews.co.nz), *Gourmet Traveller* (http://gourmet.ninemsn.com.au/gourmet-traveller) and *New Scientist* (www.newscientist.com).

Specialised journals such as *Crikey.com* (www.crikey. com.au) and e-journal On Line Opinion (www. onlineopinion. com.au) contain articles targeted to a particular readership or centred around a topic area.

These publications are listed in directories such as *Margaret Gee's Media Guide* (www.mediaguide.com.au), which is available through libraries in print or online format.

Some specialised magazines and journals only appear online, while others are available in both print and online formats. Public, state, special and university libraries subscribe to journals that reflect the focus of their collections.

## Broadcast programs

Transcripts and audio files from broadcast programs such as *The 7.30 Report* (www.abc.net.au/7.30), *Four Corners* (www.abc.net.au/4corners) and *Catalyst* (www.abc.net.au/ catalyst) are available from their websites.

## Newsletters

Newsletters such as the *Occupational Health News* and *Netball Victoria* are published by many institutions and associations and contain their internal news and updates on industry segments or products. These publications contain very specific information and are intended for people who know the area.

Journalists can turn information from newsletter articles into a news story or a column which will be relevant to a wide readership, as in 'Too Many e-tail Holes in the Net' (Gittins, 2000), which referred to analysis within Treasury's *Economic Roundup* to explain why few shoppers were shopping online.

You can find newsletters through *Margaret Gee's Media Guide* (as above), or through resources such as Newsletter Access (www.newsletteraccess.com). Newsletters are available in special-interest, TAFE and university libraries.

## Trade publications

Periodicals such as *Master Builder* and *Australian Dairy Farmer* contain industry-specific information. This is the place to find out about the changes, problems and current issues in a particular industry, and to locate upcoming seminars and conferences where you can make contacts with industry practitioners.

Use *Margaret Gee's Media Guide* to find trade publications. They are available in specialist and TAFE libraries where their topic is appropriate for the library's collection.

## Scholarly journals

Scholarly publications such as the *Medical Journal of Australia* (www.mja.com.au) and the *Australasian Journal of Disaster and Trauma Studies* (www.massey.ac.nz/~trauma/info/journal.htm) are often (though not always) peer-reviewed, meaning that their articles, after being written by academics, are reviewed by other experts in the field. This process means that their information is high-quality, although it may be difficult for a layperson to understand as it is intended for scholars in the field.

Rather than containing unsubstantiated opinions, features in these publications are usually based on the results of studies, research projects and well-conducted surveys, and include a bibliography of their references. However, as Stewart Fist (2000) points out, 'there is no guarantee that anything is trustworthy'. In his article, 'Watchdogs We Need to Watch', Fist claims that problems in the medical journal and peer review system have arisen from research scientists not revealing conflicts of interest arising from their multiple funding affiliations.

Medical and science journalists often find news stories by monitoring articles in scholarly journals which announce the results of research, such as 'Surgery Recovery Easier for Quitters' (Robotham, 2002), a *Sydney Morning Herald* story which was based on a journal article from the *Lancet*.

A news story from *The Australian*, 'US Ignites Corporate Health Fear' (Kerin, 2001) was based on a report published in the *Medical Journal of Australia*.

A number of medical journals, such as the *British Medical Journal* (www.bmj.com) and the *Journal of the American Medical Association* (http://jama.ama-assn.org) provide at least some of their articles for free through their websites.

The Directory of Open Access Journals (www.doaj.org) covers scholarly and scientific journals, while FreeMedicalJournals.com (www.freemedicaljournals.com) is a guide to publications that make their articles freely available. Articles from science and technology journals are included in the SciTech Daily Review (www.scitechdaily.com).

Sites for scholarly peer-reviewed journals are linked through portals such as Australian Journals Online (www.nla.gov.au/ajol) and Scholarly Journals Distributed Through the World Wide Web (http://info.lib.uh.edu/wj/webjour.html).

The National Library of New Zealand guide to journals, magazines and serials (http://webdirectory.natlib.govt.nz/dir/en/nz/news-media-and-publishing/journals-magazines-and-serials) includes scholarly and industry publications.

Specialist, TAFE and university libraries will subscribe to scholarly journals which are relevant to their collections. The names of the journals they subscribe to will be shown in their catalogues.

### E-prints

E-prints archives in universities include published and unpublished scholarly articles, as well as transcripts and conference papers. For example, Gateways to ePrints (www.library.uq.edu.au/database/eprints.html) is the University of Queensland's ePrints archive.

## EXERCISE

Find one example each of a popular magazine, a specialist journal, a newsletter, a trade publication and a scholarly journal which are focused on the same or a similar topic—for example, women, children, gardening, sailing, or gambling.

## FINDING ARTICLES IN INDEXES AND DATABASES

Any time you want to find articles from periodicals, whether the topic you are investigating is the reporting of a disaster or celebrity dieting, an efficient way to do so is to use indexes and databases.

These resources will help you find out what's been published in newspapers, magazines, industry newsletters and scholarly journals about everything from skateboard accidents to geopolitics and space travel research.

The contents of these indexes and databases are often invisible to search engines, so they have to be searched using their own retrieval software. Should you bother doing this when you can easily find so much with a search engine? Also, these resources may not be free of charge. In fact, subscriptions to large commercial indexes and databases can be very expensive.

Yes, you should, because in return for the effort and the cost involved in using their structured systems, these tools give you the security of knowing you can retrieve the relevant articles or transcripts they contain every time, providing you search effectively.

Journalist Pilita Clark (2003) says:

> The range of research tools now available to journalists has probably never been greater than it is today. My favourite is probably the exceptional (and exceptionally expensive) LexisNexis database. Its enormous range of publications has helped me find information in minutes that would otherwise have taken weeks, or might never have been found at all.

## Index types

There are many kinds of indexes, which are essentially lists of terms or topics which describe where to find information relevant to the indexed terms.

In the indexes in the back of books, the topics correspond to page numbers. In a bibliographic index such as APAIS (the Australian Public Affairs Information Service), the list of topics corresponds to references to articles about the topic. APAIS indexes articles about humanities and social sciences topics from newspapers, journal articles and conference papers.

These bibliographic indexes give a citation, which is the information you need to find the article. A typical citation includes the periodical issue number and date, the name of the article and its author. For example:

Jones, M., 'Swing revival', *Music News*, 1 August 2004.

An abstract (a brief summary of the article) is often provided with the citation.

In a bibliographic database, the full text of some or all of the articles will be provided. For example, APA-FT, or Australian Public Affairs—Full Text, is a bibliographic database which includes the full text of some of the articles indexed in APAIS.

If the articles are not provided, they can be obtained from the periodical in which they were published, a library which subscribes to the periodical, a website which contains the articles, or a full-text database.

Full-text databases contain the entire article or transcript, often with images. For example NewsText (www.newstext.com.au) is a database of articles and images from News Ltd newspapers. Articles from New Zealand news and business publications are available through Newztext (www.knowledge-basket.co.nz/kete/db/db.html).

## Index and database production

Database producers may publish and market a database of their content themselves, such as the Fairfax archive NewsStore (http://newsstore.f2.com.au/apps/newsSearch.ac), which contains the content of Fairfax publications. They could offer free access, charge a small fee to find or download each article, or charge users a subscription fee for access over a period of time.

Organisations such as media companies and research institutions may also sell their databases to other service providers. For example, the National Library of Australia produces the APA-FT bibliographic database, then sells it to Informit Online (RMIT Publishing). Informit Online packages APA-FT together with other databases to make a product called AUSTROM, which it in turn sells to libraries and other organisations.

Large commercial vendors, such as LexisNexis, Factiva Research and DIALOG, allow their subscribers to access the contents of thousands of databases of content from periodicals, law reports, industry and scholarly journals and trade newsletters. Their resources include major Australian and New Zealand newspapers and a host of other relevant publications.

Some of the major service providers which host international periodical indexes include ProQuest, SilverPlatter, Cambridge Scientific Abstracts and EBSCOHost.

## Index and database problems

Access to these vast collections of information has resulted in some problems, such as the perpetration of mistakes. Carl Cannon (2001) claims the number of journalists relying on information from databases of articles without checking their claims has caused mistakes to be repeated and spread, eventually becoming almost impossible to correct.

It is always necessary to check the facts and claims in articles elsewhere. They are someone else's report or opinion, in line with their agenda and their bias, and they need to be checked against other sources.

## Access to indexes and databases

Access to commercial databases is available to staff and students at academic libraries, to the employees of organisations which subscribe to them, and to the general public at state and public libraries.

Library websites often contain directories of indexes. One example is Indexes and Databases from the National Library of Australia (www.nla.gov.au/pathways/jnls/newsite/index.html), which includes online and offline resources.

Through the Australian Libraries Gateway (www.nla.gov.au/libraries), you can identify indexes in libraries, and contact librarians who will be happy to advise you on the best index for your needs.

Indexes covering certain periods may only be available in microfiche or print format. For example, the New South Wales State Library index to Australian material in the *Sydney Morning Herald* from 1900 to 1987 is available only in microfiche format.

## Free indexes

As well as the fee- or subscription-based services, many free or low-cost indexes are mounted on the web. These publications vary in terms of comprehensiveness and ease of use.

Some of them are excellent resources, such as INFO-QUICK (www.sl.nsw.gov.au/infoquick), the New South Wales State Library bibliographic index to the *Sydney Morning Herald* and Find Articles (www.findarticles.com), which links to articles from 900 magazines and journals. PubMed (www.pubmedcentral.nih.gov) contains citations for material published in thousands of biomedical journals, with links to some full-text articles. Other free indexes may not be comprehensive or updated regularly.

## Searching indexes

Before you begin searching an index, it is advisable to clarify as carefully as possible the precise information you need. Instead of searching for material about 'beach pollution', are you looking for pollution from sewage, stormwater or pesticides? During which period of time, and in which geographical area? Think of any catchphrases or acronyms which might be commonly used in connection with this topic or issue.

The articles in indexes are often given *subject headings* which define the topic of the article, regardless of its title. Subject headings or descriptors make it possible to find articles about a particular topic, even when your chosen search terms are not contained within the title and the articles text.

For instance, if you are researching deaths from drug overdoses, a relevant article called 'Injection Room Trial Abandoned' may contain the words 'heroin' instead of 'drugs'. It is equally likely that it could contain the words 'died' or 'did not survive' instead of 'deaths'. However, searching for the subject headings 'drug abuse' AND ('deaths' OR 'fatalities') will retrieve this article, as well as others on the same topic.

Subject headings are taken from a predefined list of terms called a thesaurus, which you can use to find appropriate subject headings for your topic.

You may also be able to search for *keywords* within the title, or within the article. A keyword search will usually produce many results, which will include some relevant articles. If you make a note of the subject headings attached to a relevant article, you can search again for articles with the same subject headings to find a smaller collection of the most relevant material.

## Using indexes

Many guides provide step-by-step instructions for using indexes. The National Library of Australia's 'How to Find Journal Articles' (www.nla.gov.au/pathways/journalarticles. html) guides users of Academic Search Premier and Australian Public Affairs—Full Text.

## Searching Factiva

Factiva (Dow Jones and Reuters) is a full-text database which contains articles from newspapers, periodicals and newswires worldwide.

To find articles about Brisbane Lord Mayor Campbell Newman, for example, open Factiva and, from the 'Search builder' page, select 'Major Australian newspapers'. Input 'Campbell Newman' as a free text search. This search will produce a list of titles of articles with a citation and a brief description of each article.

## Searching Expanded Academic ASAP Plus

If you wanted to find articles from journals about Australia's Free Trade Agreement with the United States, an excellent index for this purpose would be Expanded Academic ASAP Plus, an international index to articles about business, education, science, health, humanities and social science topics. This resource indexes thousands of periodicals, with many in full text. To use this index, select it from your library's list of databases.

From the Advanced Search screen, type in your search term, enclosing it in inverted commas: 'free trade agreement'. Enclosing a multiple-word search term in inverted commas finds citations in which this precise term appears, rather than finding citations in which these words appear separately.

Add the keywords 'Australia' and 'US', as well as the truncation symbol * to the term 'US' to retrieve articles which refer both to 'USA' and 'US'.

This search will produce a list of articles with citations, with some linked to the full text article.

## EXERCISE

Using an index such as APA-FT, Expanded Academic Index or Agricola, find a reference to an article about a current environmental issue.

## MEDLINE: SEARCHING SCHOLARLY JOURNALS

How can you find articles written by experts about the benefits and disadvantages of using particular treatments, such as naltrexone implants to treat heroin addiction? An index such as Medline allows you to find articles published in scholarly journals which announce the results of research into this treatment. Articles published in medical journals lead to many 'medical breakthrough' or 'health problem' news stories, and information from them also underpins longer features and programs.

Medline may be available through a number of host services, such as Ovid, Ebsco and ScienceDirect. It is a subscription service, so you will need to access Medline through your library's collection of databases.

After opening the service, input the search terms: <'naltrexone' and 'heroin addiction'>. The results will include a number of citations and abstracts for articles. Click on the title of the article to receive the full description, which includes the MeSH terms. These indexing terms have been chosen to describe and define this article. Once you find one article which is appropriate for you, you can find other suitable articles by clicking on the appropriate MeSH term, such as 'Naltrexone/adverse effects'.

If you find too many articles, you can limit your search by aspects including date, language type and publication. For instance, you could choose to only find articles published in the *British Medical Journal*.

How do you get the complete articles? The article in full text will be linked from some citations. There may also be a link to your library's catalogue so you can see whether your library holds the journal in which this article was printed. If not, you may need to request the article using the inter-library loan service offered by your library.

## EXERCISE

Choose Medline and search for articles about the medical complications that can arise from tattooing, as well as drug treatments for psychotic people.

## ONLINE COMMUNITIES

In just half an hour on a mailing list you can pick up rumours, hear intimate details about the lives of strangers, be battered by extremist ranting and raving, and receive advice from top experts.

Unless access is restricted to particular groups of people, anyone with internet access may be able to partic-ipate in online communities, so the interaction on these forums is a great way to pick up a feel for what people are saying about current topics. However, extreme caution is needed because you usually have no idea of who the participants really are.

Online communities could be:

- forums or message boards on websites set up for discussion of the site's topic;
- weblogs which function as online journals and are accessed through the web;
- mailing lists that you subscribe to and participate in by email;
- chat rooms where you log on to a site and then chat online with others; or
- newsgroups where all the discussions can be read through a web browser.

There will be an online community somewhere which corresponds to your beat or special interest—probably hundreds of them.

You can put obscure research questions to community members, who could include people who are highly qualified to answer your question, although you should beware of taking their words at face value. More often, list members will point you in the right direction, towards the organisation or group with the knowledge you are looking for.

You should not on any account copy and publish anything posted to an online community without contacting the person who made the posting, establishing who they really are and their credentials, identifying yourself and asking their permission to quote them.

## Forums or message boards

Forums or message boards such as the Australia Genealogy Forum (http://genforum.genealogy.com/australia) provide a platform where users of the site can post tips and share information with like-minded people.

Message board communities can be found through BoardReader (www.boardreader.com).

## Weblogs

Weblogs (blogs) function as online journals, where people with a special interest in a subject, topic or issue post frequent updates, reviews and links to their recommended websites.

The entries can include personal observations and interpretation provided by the blogger or weblog author. Weblogs can be set up by individuals who are experts or fanatics, or on behalf of groups, organisations and publications such as newspapers.

Journoz (www.journoz.com/weblog/) provides updates for Australian journalists, while E-Media Tidbits (www.poynter. org/tidbits) focuses on the US media industry.

Find weblogs with a search in Daypop (www.daypop.com).

## Mailing lists

Mailing lists provide a way for a group of people to communicate with each other on an area of common interest, using email. Messages are sent to a central address and then automatically distributed to the in-boxes of the subscribers to the list. By subscribing to mailing lists, you can find experts and anecdotes and pick up the latest reactions on the ground and rumours about current issues.

Early hints about problems with products such as problems with new software can surface first on lists, as consumers report their experience, ask for and receive help, and report back on the outcome.

Find mailing lists through Yahoo! Groups (http://groups.yahoo.com), which hosts thousands of them, listed under broad topic headings.

You can use Ozlists (www.gu.edu.au/ozlists) to find Australian mailing lists, and locate academic lists by country through CataList (www.lsoft.com/lists/listref.html) and others through Tile.Net (http://tile.net/lists).

## Chat

Chat is usually conducted through a web browser, with all parties in the discussion online at the same time. Portals such as (Yahoo! www.yahoo.com) may offer chat rooms as part of their range of services; another host of chat rooms is Chat Seek: The Chat Only Search Engine (www.chatseek.com).

## Newsgroups

Newsgroups provide a smorgasbord of opinions, ideas, facts, impressions and disasters which can inform, stimulate and inspire you, or waste vast amounts of your time.

These collections of messages are distributed through Usenet, which moves messages from network to network, rather than to individuals through email. Newsgroup discussions are available for anyone to read and participate in through their web browser.

You can find a newsgroup for everything from professional networking to ranting against politicians through Google Groups (www.google.com). There are even groups for politicians to distribute announcements, such as nz.politics.announce.

# 7

## TRACKING DOWN THE TRUFFLES

## DATABASES, DIRECTORIES AND SEARCH ENGINES

So much information, so little time! How can you surf through the oceans of unstructured information swelling over websites to grab just what you need, without getting dumped?

It is easy to type a couple of words into a general search engine and receive links to thousands of sites that include these words, but it may be hard to find credible, up-to-date information quickly from these results. You may find better information more quickly through using databases, specialised directories or search engines which focus on a particular area.

Databases are all around you, and you are already using them if you check the phone book to find a place to eat or to get your car fixed. They are collections of information organised in some systematic way to facilitate its retrieval.

Journalist Pilita Clark (2003) says:

> For me, the one major benefit of the internet has been the access it provides to many databases, from *Hansard* to the Australian Electoral Commission or the Australian Securities and Investment Commission. It also makes it easier to receive regular updates via email on, for

example, daily court lists or corporate filings. Many news stories are generated through such services and I would strongly recommend them for beginning journalists.

## Quality from within

Although you may find databases online, the entries in the fields of information which make up dynamically generated databases may be inaccessible to the automated programs that compile search engine indexes from words on linked web pages.

For this reason, databases are known as the 'invisible web'—their content may be invisible to search engines. You may need to go into them to find and retrieve items from deep within their structure and, possibly, pay a fee to use them.

However, the advantage of structured databases is that they tend to contain high-quality resources, they are updated frequently and their retrieval methods provide the security of knowing you can find all the relevant material they hold.

*Bibliographic* databases such as ABI/Inform could include references to journal articles, conference papers and research reports.

Full-text databases may contain articles, books, legislation, company records, statistical records and graphics such as photographs or maps. For example, paintings and other images can be viewed at Timeframes (http://timeframes1. natlib.govt.nz), a database of heritage images from the Alexander Turnbull Library, a division of the National Library of New Zealand.

Some databases may only be available in *microfiche or print format*. For instance, the Australian Electoral Commission's electoral roll is available to the public through its offices in microfiche format.

## Specialised directories

Directories or subject guides list selected resources in some logical way, often under categories of people, associations, products or websites.

In print or electronic format, directories provide key facts and contact information. The contents of the best directories have been selected by experts in the area, thus supplying some quality control over their resources.

An industry directory is the place to find people involved in a particular line of work. For example, companies and individuals involved in the media, arts and film industries are listed in the *Australian Media Facilities Directory* (http://orion.amfd.com.au/main.htm), and you can find public servants and politicians through directories such as the *Queensland Local Government Directory* (www.lgp.qld.gov.au/applications/lg Directory/).

To find and contact people and organisations, *telephone directories* such as *White Pages* (Telstra Australia) (www.sensis.com.au) and New Zealand *White Pages* (www.whitepages.co.nz) are the first tools of choice.

To find people with particular abilities or trades—for example, horse breeders or organisations such as genealogical societies—start with the *Yellow Pages* (Telstra Australia) (www.yellowpages.com.au) or New Zealand *Yellow Pages* (www.yellowpages.co.nz).

*Professional directories* list practitioners in a particular field, while *Margaret Gee's Australian Media Guide* (www.mediaguide.com.au) lists contact details for media businesses, journalists and regulatory bodies.

Contact details for government and business organisations are available through the *Government and Business Associations Directory* (www.business.gov.au/BEP2002/GBDirectory/GBDirList), while the *Black Pages* (www.black-pages.com.au) lists Indigenous business and community enterprises in Australia.

*Biographical directories* cover people in government, the armed forces, community groups and business. One of the best known, *Who's Who in Australia* (Information Australia, Melbourne), includes details such as date of birth, marital status, education, career history and recreational interests for performers, public servants and other identities. The *New Zealand Business Who's Who* (www.nzbww.co.nz) lists directors with their companies' details.

*Business directories* such as *Who Owns Whom* (Dun & Bradstreet Ltd, UK) list the directors, executives, subsidiaries and business activities of public and some private companies.

If you are about to hit the road on the research trail, find your way with a *street directory* such as *Gregory's Darwin and Central Australia*, *Melway Greater Melbourne* or the *UBD Brisbane*. Use Whereis Online (www.whereis.com.au) to find maps and directions, or plan your trip using the RACQ's travel planner (www.racq.com.au).

*Gateway directories* or portals such as the Internet Information Sources for Australian Journalists (www.journoz.com) collect lists of resources under topics. Australian Sport (www.ausport.gov.au) combines sporting information, services and links to major sporting bodies, while Education.gov.au (www.education.gov.au) includes all levels of education.

## Access

Directories and databases may be freely available through the web. However, some of the most useful must be paid for, in which case they may be available through libraries.

Individual databases may be packaged together and offered on a subscription basis by vendors such as Lexis-Nexis and DIALOG. With one search, subscribers to these services can access the contents of thousands of periodicals, collections of legislation and company information.

Access to large commercial databases is available to staff and students through academic libraries, to the employees of organisations and companies which subscribe to them and to the general public through state and public libraries. See the Australian Libraries Gateway (www.nla.gov.au/libraries) to find library holdings and to consult librarians for advice about databases.

Libraries' websites often include a list of databases, such as Indexes and Databases (www.nla.gov.au/pathways/jnls/newsite/index.html), the National Library of Australia's subject listing, which includes online and offline resources.

## Specialised search engines

Specialised search engines index content from particular kinds of sites. For instance, if you are looking for science-based material or software, or you want to retrieve sources from a particular country, a search engine which indexes only this material may be faster than a general search engine.

Search engines which focus on news material include Google.news (http://news.google.com), News Trawler (www.newstrawler.com) and Daypop (www.daypop.com), which includes news, weblogs and RS feeds.

Two search engines which focus on Australian and New Zealand material are Anzwers (http://au.anzwers.yahoo.com) and Sensis (www.sensis.com.au).

Alphasearch (www.alphasearch.org) is a directory of search engines, with links to many specialised search engines.

## Using search engines

There are differences in the way search engines index and retrieve material, but they also share many features. Guides such as the Infopeople Search Engines Quick Guide (http://infopeople.org/search/guide.html) give you a succinct list of the main features of some popular engines. Some tips for using search engines successfully follow. For more extensive information, see the 'Help' section on the search engine you are using.

First, use the most specific search terms you can, such as people's names, place names and scientific or medical terms.

Second, search for phrases or parts of sentences rather than keywords, so your search terms are both specific and appear in some context, such as 'treatment for bowel cancer' or 'opposed the Free Trade Agreement'. The articles and documents that will be most useful to you are more likely to have this text string near the beginning and/or repeated within the text.

Third, add some extra search terms in order to find material from particular kinds of sites. For example, adding 'site:au' or 'site:nz' in a Google search will find only materials from Australian or New Zealand sites.

## EXERCISE

1   From a directory, find the name of the president of an association which represents childcare workers in the Northern Territory.
2   Find the figures for donations to the major parties in the last election. Who were the three top donors, and how much did they donate to either or both parties?
3   Using a directory, find some information about Morocco: its size, climate and population, language, GDP, currency and the name of its president/prime minister.

## REFERENCE RESOURCES

Reference resources are some of the most widely used and available research tools. Encyclopaedias and dictionaries are great for basic and specialised information about unfamiliar topics, and telephone directories and street directories can be surprisingly helpful. Most libraries have a collection of reference resources for quick access, which you can browse using classification numbers as a location guide; alternatively, you can use the library's catalogue to find what you need.

### Ask a reference question

As well as looking yourself, you can ask librarians for the answers to reference questions, such as 'What is the currency of Vietnam?' This service is usually offered to the public by state libraries and may be offered by large public libraries.

Libraries may offer their reference services in person, by telephone or online via email, the web or chat sessions. You can contact reference librarians through the Australian Libraries Gateway (www.nla.gov.au/libraries).

### Reference directories and portals

Comprehensive Australian portals include Basic Reference Sites (www.journoz.com) from the *OzGuide for Australian Journalists*, Reference & Current Affairs (www.nla.gov. au/pathways/jnls/newsite/browse/refca.html#Reference) from the National Library of Australia and *Reference and Research Tools* (www.aph.gov.au/library/intguide/gen/genref. htm) from the Department of the Parliamentary Library.

The National Library of New Zealand maintains a General and Reference portal at (http://webdirectory.natlib. govt.nz/dir/en/nz/general-and-reference).

## Reference categories

The main categories of reference materials, with examples that illustrate their use, are as follows:

- *Almanacs* are chronologies of the year's events. They provide lists of disasters/crimes, and so forth by region, as well as political summaries. The information is often presented in condensed form, such as that contained in the *Guinness Book of World Records* (www.guinness worldrecords.com) and the *Wisden Cricketers' Almanack.*
- *Atlases* such as *Geographica: The Complete Illustrated Reference to Australia and the World* (Bateman, NZ) can contain historical, economic, social, political and environmental information, as well as maps. The *Australian Coastal Atlas* (www.ea.gov.au/coasts/atlas) includes mapping tools which enable you to produce custom maps.
- *Calendars* organise events in time. For example, the Australian Culture and Recreation Calendar (www.cultureandrecreation.gov.au) lists events under categories such as 'New Media Arts'.
- *Catalogues* are lists of items arranged in alphabetical order. Like most library catalogues, The Pictures Catalogue for the National Library of Australia's Pictorial Collection (www.nla.gov.au/catalogue/pictures) contains descriptions of the contents of its collection.
- *Converters* and *calculators* such as the Time Zone converter (www.timezoneconverter.com) and the Universal Currency Converter (www.xe.net/ucc) are tools for converting different currencies and performing mathematical calculations.
- *Dictionaries* such as the *Macquarie Dictionary* (www.macquariedictionary.com.au) explain the words of

a language, giving each word's meaning, derivation and pronunciation.

- *Specialist dictionaries* define and explain a particular area, sometimes visually as well as verbally. They include the specialised language or jargon used for the activity or occupation. For example, the *McGraw-Hill Dictionary of Scientific and Technical Terms* (www.access-science.com/Dictionary) explains terms and also gives their pronunciation.

- *Encyclopaedias* contain information, prepared by experts, on all parts of a topic. They are an ideal place to find a complicated topic explained in simple language. Use a general encyclopaedia such as the *Encyclopædia Britannica* to check a fact such as the birth rate for a country. The online *Encyclopædia Britannica* (www.britannica.com) is subscription-based.

- *Specialist encyclopaedias* contain information on a special field for which experts have prepared outlines of facts and research findings, usually in language suitable for a layperson. For example, the *Merck Index: An Encyclopedia of Chemicals, Drugs and Biologicals* (www.merck.com/pubs) contains cross-indexed information about chemicals.

- For quick facts and records, see *Factbooks* and *Surveys* such as *Country Briefings* (www.economist.com/countries), prepared by The Economist Intelligence Unit, and *The World Factbook* (www.odci.gov/cia/publications/factbook) from the CIA.

- *Gazetteers* such as *The Great Australia Gazetteer* (www.australiagazetteer.com) are geographical dictionaries with statistical or historical information.

- *Glossaries* define terms and abbreviations for a particular field. For example, a Glossary of Rhetorical Terms with Examples (www.uky.edu/ArtsSciences/Classics/rhetoric.

html) explains language concepts such as metaphor, hyperbole, etc.

- *Handbooks* or *manuals* contain concise information for practitioners about core aspects of a particular area or activity. They are useful for quick grounding in a topic with which you are unfamiliar. For example, the *Drugs in Sport Handbook* (Australian Sports Drug Agency, ACT) shows which drugs are banned for athletes.

- *Indexes* show the locations of specialised categories of information. For example, to find Australian folk songs try the Index of Australian Folk Songs (www.crixa. com/muse/songnet/songs.html). Iwidex (www.auckland library.co.nz/process.asp?pageurl=/explore/maori/ trrmiwidex.html) indexes sources of information on tribal history held in Auckland City libraries.

- *News summaries* are weekly or monthly digests of news events, listed by date, country or subjects. They are an excellent way of checking when events occurred and the names of the main players. Two of the best-known news summaries are *Facts on File World News Digest* (www.facts.com/online-wnd.htm) and *Keesing's Record of World Events* (Longman, London), in print, online by subscription.

- Look up *quotations* quickly with guides such as *Bartlett's Familiar Quotations* (www.bartleby.com/100).

- *Standards* are the specifications which must be met when articles are manufactured—the construction method or process which is set by an official body. For example, Food Standards Australia New Zealand (www.foodstandards.gov.au) specifies the standards which apply to foods which are produced or imported for sale there. Most of the Australian Standards are available through public and TAFE libraries, or online by subscription, as is Standards Australia's catalogue (www.standards.com.au/catalogue/script/search.asp).

- *Thesauri* provide synonyms and antonyms. One of the best known is *Roget's Thesaurus* (www.thesaurus.com/thesaurus).
- *Yearbooks* contain overviews of a particular year's events for an industry, geographical area, or profession, with statistics summarising social and economic data. *The B&T Yearbook* (Reed Business Information, Sydney, 2004) includes information relevant to advertising, media and marketing companies. *The New Zealand Official Yearbook 2002* is produced by Statistics New Zealand, while *The World Guide 2001/2002* CD-ROM is a reference to developing countries.

## EXERCISE

You are about to leave for Vietnam to research a documentary about access to health services in that country. Using reference resources, research the biggest health problems, health facilities and the treatments available.

## LIBRARIES

Although they may never walk through their doors, politicians, public servants and political activists all rely on libraries to link them to the information they need.

The advantage of accessing information through a library is that their resources are packaged to meet the needs of their clients, catalogued under subject headings or organised in directories and information gateways so they can be found and retrieved.

Although many resources are online, many more are available offline, and a multitude of valuable resources can only be located through libraries. Stan Correy, of ABC Radio's *Background Briefing* program says (2004):

In a way the internet has ruined research because people think if they put in a few words to a search engine they have found everything but they certainly have not. I use periodical indexes, library catalogues and full-text databases of magazine articles. And serendipity, browsing through the magazines in subject areas I'm interested in, at the Fisher Library at the University of Sydney. It's handy that I know the Dewey system so I can go straight to the subject areas.

If you are looking for specialised information, you can consult a librarian with knowledge of the topic you are researching. Even if their library does not contain the item, librarians can direct you to the collections or databases that are likely to hold or have indexed the resource you are seeking.

## Depository libraries

If you are trying to track down a hard-to-find book or government report, try the catalogue of the appropriate depository library. State public libraries, the National Library and some public libraries are depository libraries, meaning that it is obligatory for a copy of certain categories of publication to be deposited in these libraries.

## Libraries defined

The collections of the huge *university libraries* are specialised collections of great depth that support the particular areas taught by that university. These libraries offer excellent access to databases, as well as books, videos and specialised journals. People without an affiliation with the university can usually use these libraries to some extent by visiting in person, and by consulting their catalogues and other online resources.

*TAFE libraries* also collect resources in specialised areas, including business and management topics as well as trade areas, to support their educational programs. For example, the Northern Sydney TAFE library collection includes resources dealing with accounting and management, as well as automotive mechanics, carpentry, plumbing, hairdressing and a collection of Australian Standards. Visitors can usually consult their resources in person.

*State and public libraries* aim to have a little of everything, in keeping with their service mission to meet the needs of the general public. They try to make their services easily available to the public. For example, digitised historical material from the J.S. Battye Library of West Australian History, including oral history recordings and photographs, is available online.

These libraries may offer *information centres* which bring together resources for a particular area. For example, the State Library of New South Wales (www.sl.nsw.gov.au) contains a legal centre, health centre and family history centre.

A *virtual library* such as Infomine (http://infomine. ucr.edu) consists of resources collected with a particular user population in mind. These libraries may link the resources of many information services and tend to include specialised databases, reference works and subject guides.

*Special libraries* in government or private research agencies and corporate environments provide highly specialised information services to people making public policy and business decisions. For example, the Aboriginal and Torres Strait Islander Studies Library (www.aiatsis. gov.au) collects materials which support Aboriginal and Torres Strait Islander studies.

Parliaments, museums, legal firms, unions, professional

associations, clubs, manufacturers, hospitals and government departments may have their own libraries, but members of the public usually need to negotiate access to the holdings of these special libraries.

*Parliamentary libraries* employ researchers who write high-quality analytical reports about the issues of the day. For example, the publications produced by the Information and Analytical Services of the Parliamentary Library of the Commonwealth of Australia (www.aph.gov.au/library/index.htm) include Bills Digests, Background Papers, Current Issues Briefs and E-briefs which provide background and commentary on current topics. Its 'Crime and Candidacy' Current Issues Brief, for example, outlines the issues related to persons with a criminal record standing for political office. (Parliamentary Library Current Issues Brief, no. 22, 2002–03, www.aph.gov.au/library/pubs/cib/2002–03/ 03cib22.pdf). These resources may be available through their websites or they could be in university and other libraries in hard copy.

*Subscription libraries* such as the Questia Online Library of Books and Journals (www.questia.com) and Ebrary.com are private enterprise research services that grant their subscribers access to thousands of volumes.

## Special collections

Libraries may contain special collections focused on regional information, local history or political groups. Their holdings may include rare books, pamphlets, posters, films, videos, notices, clothing and the agendas of meetings.

For example, the Fryer Library at The University of Queensland holds a collection of political and election ephemera gathered from activists, candidates and parties, such as pamphlets, posters, how-to-vote cards, brochures, badges and t-shirts.

## Finding libraries

The Australian Libraries Gateway (ALG) (www.nla.gv.au/libraries) is a directory service for public, state, TAFE, university and special libraries in Australia.

To locate libraries in New Zealand, General and Reference Libraries (http://webdirectory.natlib.govt.nz/dir/en/nz/general-and-reference/libraries) is a comprehensive guide.

## Library sections

In the *reference* collections of libraries, you can find a quick statistic, check the spelling of a word or get an overview of a topic. Reference materials are intended to be consulted rather than read in their entirety.

Librarians at the National Library and the State Libraries will answer *information queries* from members of the public in person and by telephone and email.

The *general/lending collection* will usually have books, multimedia material, maps, kits, etc. and more up-to-date material will be found here. Periodicals such as magazines and journals may be located here or in their own collection.

While the catalogue will tell you what periodicals the library holds and where to find them, an index will tell you in which issue of which periodical a particular article appears, or at which conference a particular paper was delivered. See the section on 'Finding articles in indexes and databases' in Chapter 6.

You can access an item held by another library through an *interlibrary loan*, whether it is borrowing a video held by another library or requesting a photocopy of an article from a journal held elsewhere.

You may be able to use Kinetica, the Australian Library

Network, in your local library to find books, periodicals and other materials held in other libraries.

## Locating resources

To find information through libraries, you can navigate a path to the resources you need by:

- finding items in the catalogue by looking under their title, author or their subject and getting a location for them; or
- browsing the shelves of the library, in person or online, using the classification system to locate material on a topic.

Most library catalogues contain a menu from which you can choose the field/s to search, such as author, title, subject heading or keyword. Check the 'help' screen to find how the catalogue works.

Library catalogue entries usually contain the author's full name, the title, the edition, the place and date of publication, the subject headings, the publisher's name, the number of volumes (if there are more than one) and the classification number or symbol.

The subject headings or descriptors which describe the content of the resource are selected from a controlled vocabulary, often the Library of Congress Subject Headings. When one library catalogues a book using a particular subject heading other libraries will usually follow suit, so once you find a few resources on your topic you can use the same subject headings to find more materials elsewhere.

If you cannot find anything, it may help to phrase your topic in different ways and contexts and consider searching under broader terms, synonyms, antonyms, or related terms. If you are finding too many records, try searching under narrower terms than those you initially entered.

You can also reduce the number of records retrieved by using Boolean searching to combine and exclude terms. For example, entering 'industrial relations' AND 'law' means that each record retrieved will contain both search terms.

## Finding resources on the shelf

The *call numbers* given with the catalogue entries guide you to the resource's location on the shelves in the reference, general and other collections.

The same subject may be classified in more than one place. For example, material dealing with 'the family' may be with material classified under ethics, religion, sociology, social customs, home economics, genealogy, psychology, or law.

Two of the most commonly used classification systems are the Dewey system, commonly used in public libraries, and the Library of Congress system, often used in university libraries.

The broad locations for both systems are shown in Table 7.1:

**Table 7.1  Library locations by classification system**

| Topics | Dewey | Library of Congress |
|---|---|---|
| Agriculture | 630–9 | S |
| Architecture | 720–9 | NA |
| Arts | 700–99 | M, N |
| Astronomy | 520–9 | QB |
| Atlases | 911 | G |
| Biographical directories | 920–9 | CT |
| Business | 330–82, 650–9 | HF–HG |
| Communications | 383–4 | P |

| | | |
|---|---|---|
| Computer science | 004–6, 651.8, 652.5 | QA |
| Cookery | 641 | TX |
| Dictionaries | 400–99 | AG |
| Economics | 330–9 | HB–HC |
| Education | 370–9 | L |
| Encyclopaedias | 030–9 | AE |
| Environment | 304, 333, 363, 574 | GE |
| Family | 305 | HQ |
| Film, TV | 302 | PN |
| Gardening | 635 | SB |
| Genealogy | 920–9 | CS |
| Geography | 910–19 | G |
| Graphic art | 760 | NC |
| Health, medicine | 610–19 | R |
| History | 930–99 | E–F |
| Indigenous studies | 323 | GN |
| Internet | 004 | TK |
| Journalism | 070–9 | PN |
| Law | 340–9 | K |
| Literature | 800–99 | P |
| Management | 650–9 | HD |
| Manufacturing | 670–89 | HD |
| Maps | 911 | GB |
| Music | 780–9 | M |
| Performing arts | 790–2 | PN |
| Photography | 770–9 | TR |
| Political science | 320–9 | J |
| Psychology | 150–9 | BF |
| Public administration | 350–4 | JF |
| Religion | 200–99 | BL |
| Science | 500–99 | Q |
| Social problems | 360 | HV |
| Sport | 793–9 | GV |
| Statistics | 310–19 | HA |

| Street directories | 910–19 | G |
| Technology | 600–99 | T0 |
| Theatre, TV, dance | 790–2 | PN |
| Travel | 910–19 | G |

Within each collection, items are arranged in order by their classification number. Dewey Decimal Classification (DDC) numbers are decimal numbers, so 658.1235 will be shelved between 658.122 and 658.124. Following the DDC number, items are shelved alphabetically and/or numerically by an alphabetic sequence and/or running numbers. (Running numbers are whole numbers.)

Once you find an appropriate book or video, by searching again by its call number in the catalogue you can find other relevant items located close by, thus browsing the library shelves online.

## EXERCISE

Find a special library that collects resources about sports drugs, schizophrenia, beach ecology, the media or a major religion.

## ARCHIVES

Some of the biggest page one headlines in major newspapers appear on stories which are sourced to archive records.

The *Commonwealth Archives Act 1983* provides for public access to most documents from Commonwealth government bodies after 30 years have elapsed. Subject to exemptions which are set out in the Act, sensitive documents—such as Cabinet submissions which reveal the background to major political decisions—are released to public scrutiny at the beginning of each year.

Typical of the stories which result is 'Revealed: Secret Offer for Troops to Vietnam' which appeared in *The Australian* on 1 January 1996 (Stewart, 1996), offering reinterpretation and reassessment of the relevant events.

These reports, however, are only the most obvious use of archive records. Archives are an invaluable historical tool for documentary research, and an exciting way for family historians to turn up original records about individuals.

## Archive materials

Public archives hold the records from public offices and courts that must be stored permanently for official purposes. They contain materials such as reports, letters, maps, files, photographs, posters, sound recordings and videotapes.

Commonwealth government archives can contain everything from sensitive material documenting the real reasons for participating in wars to the films made by government departments.

This material can be drawn on to research books and documentaries. For example, the films made by government departments of the 1950s Australia Car Trials were used to produce the documentary *REDeX Round Australia Car Trials 1953, 54 and 55*.

Inquest reports, the staff files of public servants, war diaries and medical records, probate records, and the personal files kept on people who arrived as immigrants may be retained in archives.

As well as documents, the excitement of live performances lives on in archives. The ScreenSound Australia News Archive (www.screensound.gov.au) contains classic radio serials and comedy sketches, recordings of Australian Rock-'n'Roll musicians and interviews with the creators of early television.

Online publications, including electronic journals, organisational sites, government documents and ephemera, have been archived by the National Library of Australia within the PANDORA Archive (http://pandora.nla.gov.au/index.html).

## Types of archives

The Australian Archives are the Commonwealth government's main archival institution, with records of Commonwealth government departments and other agencies dating back to Federation in 1901. With its head office in Canberra, there is an office of the Australian Archives in each of the state capital cities, as well as in Darwin and Townsville.

Australian states and the Northern Territory have also created Public Archives collections, organised along the same lines as those of the Commonwealth.

As well as government agencies, organisations such as trade unions, universities, public companies and private individuals may all create and maintain archives. Union collections can be assessed through Australian Trade Union Archives (www.atua.org.au/atua.htm).

The archives of organisations will contain their internal records, such as minutes of meetings, lists of office-holders from particular periods, campaign records, policies and letters.

## Finding archived records

Finding records in archives is a different process from accessing library material. Archival materials from each individual or agency are kept together in 'record groups' and/or 'record series' in the same sequence and filing system in which they were originally created by the department or agency.

Begin your search by identifying which agencies might

have created the records and when the material was probably assembled. You can then use the original indexes created by these agencies to identify the particular files you are seeking.

Researchers can access the complete Australian Archives database in the public reading rooms of the Archives, and in the Australian War Memorial in Canberra. This database has information about what records have been created and where they are located. Query terms include keywords, registration numbers, date range, location and the name of the agency which created the records.

Archives guides and fact sheets are available in the reading rooms and on the Australian Archives website. These finding aids help to locate specialised material—for instance, records about Aboriginal and Torres Strait Islander people.

At the National Archives of Australia (www.naa.gov.au), a keyword search of the item titles on the database will give you a broad indication of the records available on a particular topic, and lead you to series that are likely to contain records relevant to your search. It will also indicate the office of the Australian Archives in which they are located.

**Finding archives**

The main Australian and New Zealand government archives are:
- Archives of Australia: www.archivenet.gov.au/archives. html;
- State Records of New South Wales: www.records.nsw. gov.au;
- Public Records Office of Victoria: www.prov.vic.gov.au/access.htm;
- Queensland State Archives: www.archives.qld.gov.au;

- State Records of Western Australia: www.sro.wa.gov.au;
- Archives of South Australia: www.archives.sa.gov.au;
- Archive Service of Northern Territory: www.nt.gov.au/nta;
- Archives Office of Tasmania: www.archives.tas.gov.au;
- Archives of New Zealand: www.archives.govt.nz.

The Directory of Archives in Australia (www.archivists. org.au/directory/asa_dir.htm) contains contact information for 450 archival repositories, while non-government archives are included within the Register of Australian Archives and Manuscripts (RAAM) database (www.nla.gov.au/raam).

The Gateway to Archives in New Zealand (http:// marvin.otago.ac.nz/gateways/index.htm) includes government and non-government archives.

# 8

## SCRATCHING UP THE NUMBERS AND CRUNCHING THEM

## STATISTICS

How many tourists drowned on Australian beaches last year? Which football code attracts the biggest crowds? How much money do people gamble away each year? Is street crime really getting worse, or is it actually pretty safe out there?

There's a seductive allure about hard facts, and a startling figure like private school enrolments increasing at 20 times the rate of government schools just needs a few quotes to become a strong story, as in 'Private School Enrolments Boom' (Jackman, 2003a). The arguments in a feature acquire credibility by being backed up with statistics from an authoritative source.

The ugly side of statistics is that they can be very slippery, so it is wise to understand how the figures were produced. For example, if the sample sizes used for surveys are very small, the results can be meaningless. See 'Querying the figures' in Chapter 1 for information about survey practices.

To understand statistics, *The Electronic Statistics Textbook*, The Statistics Home Page (www.statsoft.com/

textbook/stathome.html) covers basic and complex concepts, while Statistics Every Writer Should Know (http://robertniles. com) explains sample sizes, margin of error, data analysis, standard deviation and normal distribution.

## Using figures in stories

David Dale of the *Sydney Morning Herald* finds that unexpected figures can produce great stories by using good-quality statistics:

> My role at the *Sydney Morning Herald* is to write about the things Australians do in large numbers, to tell readers 'Here's what we like'. Everyone is interested in whether they are the same as or different from everyone else. So I look at every source of data, from TV ratings to wheat consumption figures.
>
> I saw an Australian Bureau of Statistics report called 'Mental Health' in early December 2003, based on a survey of our attitudes to our own sanity. The respondents were asked to rate their level of happiness, which is really the ultimate question, and the majority of Australians had responded in the happy end. I took it home to read overnight, as I often do.
>
> The survey was based on a huge sample—18 000 people. The sample sizes used in ABS reports usually satisfy normal criteria, but I always check this. Journalists get rubbish from PR companies sent to them every day, based on alleged 'surveys', but it's usually unreliable data because the sample size is too small, or the questions were not asked in the right way, or the sample was self-selected and therefore not representative.
>
> I always try to get extra information to develop the story so I rang the researcher and she said she had other

data that had not been included in the report and which she was keen to make known—what lifestyle factors correlated with the highest and lowest happiness. With the extra material, this became the front page story 'The Secret Sydney Recipe for Earthly Delights', which was published in the *Sydney Morning Herald* on 22 December 2003.

## ABS statistics

The Australian Bureau of Statistics (ABS) (www.abs.gov.au) is the official compiler of statistics for the Commonwealth and state governments of Australia. The ABS produces statistics on a wide variety of social and economic topics, such as imports, exports, demography and manufacturing.

ABS figures produce stories about changes in birth and death rates, the effects of economic reforms and labour market changes, health and diseases and the effect of our foreign debt.

Every three months, news stories are built on the release of the latest ABS *Consumer Price Index* (CPI), which records the changes in the price of a basket of goods and services over time for the eight capital cities.

Most ABS statistical bulletins, such as *Australian Social Trends*, are published regularly—weekly, monthly or quarterly—for each subject number.

ABS yearbooks provide a comprehensive annual overview of economic and social conditions in Australia. Online, the material in *Year Book Australia* appears as *Australia Now: A Statistical Profile*. Similar collections of statistics are produced for the state governments.

*ABS Themes* include summaries for each Australian state and territory, as well as collecting their data under subject headings such as 'Mining' and 'Health'.

## The census

Every five years, pages of stories announce the release of the findings of the *Australian Census of Population and Housing*, which is published by the ABS. These are the stories announcing that Australians are growing older, fewer of them are getting married and, after English, the language most often spoken at home is Chinese.

The Census Basic Community Profiles provide tables of raw data in Excel spreadsheets which contain the key characteristics of a particular geographic area, such as Melbourne. *CLIB 2001* has all the data from the Community Profile series, the working population and Indigenous profiles, and so on, as Excel spreadsheets. This chargeable resource is often available in libraries through the Library Extension Program.

Another chargeable resource, *CDATA 2001*, combines demographic information about Australia's population with MapInfo software to demonstrate the demographic and social characteristics of a selected area.

Statistics New Zealand (www.stats.govt.nz) is the place to locate official New Zealand statistics and census information.

Australian Bureau of Statistics information is available online, in CD-ROM format and in many libraries.

The ABS statistical bulletins and the Bureau's other freely available publications are only a subset of its collection. To obtain access to the full ABS collection, including AusStats, you need to pay. However, access to AusStats is available to the staff and students of universities in Australia through their libraries, and to public and TAFE library users through the ABS's Library Extension Program.

The AusStats web-based service includes:

- ABS Time Series—which enables comparisons such as

contrasting the numbers of unemployed now with those of 20 years ago;

- multi-dimensional datasets in SuperTABLE format, which are multiple cross-classified data items from ABS collections;
- Community Profiles compiled from the census data;
- *Australia Now*, a statistical summary of Australia; and
- the Statistical Concepts Library—standard ABS classifications and survey documentation.

You can search all pages on the AusStats site using the search engine, by keywords. Using the Boolean operations 'AND', 'OR' and 'AND NOT' will create more precise searches.

## Other sources of statistics

Other sources of good-quality statistics include government authorities, research institutes and organisations such as unions and charities.

For example, the Bureau of Tourism Research (www.btr.gov.au) publishes tourism statistics, and the Reserve Bank (www.rba.gov.au) produces the weekly Statement of Liabilities and Assets, as well as the daily exchange rate.

Data published by the National Centre for Social and Economic Modelling (www.natsem.canberra.edu.au) often back up stories about income inequality—how much richer the top end of town is getting and how far those at the other end of the scale are sinking.

Data produced by business include the ANZ Job Advertisement Series, a monthly indicator on the state of the job market in Australia, published by the ANZ Bank.

Collections of links to statistical information include

Economic Indicators on the Internet (www.aph.gov.au/ library/intguide/STATS/ecindicators.htm) and Statistical Resources (www.aph.gov.au/library/intguide/stats/index.htm), both from the Parliamentary Library, as well as the National Library's Australian Statistical Internet Sites (www.nla.gov. au/oz/stats.html) and the OzGuide's Statistics section (www.journoz.com/stats.html).

Each state government has its own statistics collection, such as the Queensland Office of Economic and Statistical Research (www.oesr.qld.gov.au/views/statistics/stats_home. htm). You can navigate to those produced by the other states through www.gov.au.

## International statistics

International statistics are collected in compilations such as OFFSTATS Official Statistics on the Web (www2.auckland. ac.nz/lbr/stats/offstats/OFFSTATSmain.htm), from the University of Auckland Library. Statistical Resources on the Web (www.lib.umich.edu/govdocs/stats.html) also includes worldwide resources. The World Wide Web Virtual Library collection, Statistics (www.stat.ufl.edu/vlib/statistics.html) is another extensive collection.

## EXERCISE

Find recent child abuse reporting statistics, from a government source.

## COMPUTER-ASSISTED REPORTING/DATA ANALYSIS

### Graham Cairns

How can you tell a story that includes figures in such a way that your readers or listeners will understand their significance? Crunching numbers together and analysing them can transform basic data so their significance can easily be understood.

Very often, you need to combine different sets of figures to make sense of them. If the raw number of burglaries in a particular town goes right up, we need to know whether the population has also risen so we don't misinterpret the significance of the rise. Or changes in the rates of break-and-enters may turn out to correspond to changes in the cost of heroin.

Using spreadsheet programs such as Excel, it is also possible to produce quickly the nifty graphs, pie charts and other diagrams that make the figures and diagrams in an news story much easier to comprehend.

Mathematical savants are people who have an uncanny ability to perform complex calculations in their heads, quickly and correctly each time. Most of us marvel at their abilities, but haven't got a hope of emulating them.

That's where spreadsheets come in. Number-crunching is what spreadsheets do best. They perform multiple calculations, each one dependent on the calculation before it. But spreadsheets aren't just overblown electronic calculators. They are to calculators what a Ferrari is to a billy-cart. Both have four wheels, steering and some form of propulsion, but only one allows you to travel in style.

A spreadsheet is a piece of software that performs calculations for you—but, more importantly, it allows you to change one piece of your data and see what the results of doing so would be. In essence, then, spreadsheets are a tool to show 'what-if' calculations.

For example, you might enter the number of motoring fatalities in a given year. You might also enter the number of deaths involving cars with airbags. By hypothetically changing the number of vehicles with airbags, it is possible to see what impact that might have had on the overall fatality rate.

Of course, a spreadsheet can't write your story for you, and you need to consider all available data. In the case of airbag use versus fatalities, the very success of airbags skews the figures. As economist Steven Levitt points out in his paper 'Sample Selection in the Estimation of Air Bag and Seat Belt Effectiveness':

> Measurement of seat belt and air bag effectiveness is complicated by the fact that systematic data are collected only for crashes in which a fatality occurs. These data suffer from sample selection since seat belt and air bag usage influences survival rates which in turn determine whether a crash is included in the sample.

So, you should always question whether the result of your number-crunching seems too good to be true. If it looks that way, it probably is!

Throughout the rest of this section, I'll use Microsoft Excel spreadsheets because they are (at the time of writing) the most popular spreadsheet in use in newsrooms around the world, and because most other spreadsheets emulate Excel's layout in many ways.

So let's look at what makes up a spreadsheet. A typical Excel spreadsheet has cells, rows, columns, a menu bar, toolbars and a formula bar (see Figure 1).

**Figure 1**

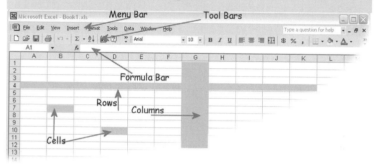

The *cell* is the basic building block of a spreadsheet. Each cell contains an individual piece of data. It might be the number of small cars with driver's-side airbags, or the total number of cars involved in accidents, or even a text label to identify the figures in cells below it. It can contain letters, or numbers, or formulae—and it is these formulae that make spreadsheets so useful.

The following are just some examples: an interactive tutorial with 'real-life' figures is provided later.

A *formula* might be a simple addition such as '=sum(g1:g12)', which means 'add all the figures in Column G, from Cell G12 to cell G12, and put the result here'. Or, it might be a more complicated one, such as '=average(a4:k4,b7,d10)', which adds all the numbers in Row 4, from a4 to k4, plus the numbers in Cells b7 and d10, and then divides them by the number of cells that contain numbers (this means that if a cell is blank, or has text in it, it is not included in the calculation).

You can type formulae directly into a cell, or you can click on a cell and type into the formula bar. The F2 function key will put you in 'edit' mode, ready to use the keyboard 'arrows'. It is important to note that a formula must begin with an equals sign (=), otherwise it will be treated as text, not as a formula.

The *menu bars* are typical of Microsoft Windows, but the *toolbars* contain some functions not found in any other program.

One is the *autosum* function. It looks like a stylised 'E' or the Greek capital sigma. Its function is, as the name suggests, to add a group of figures automatically. If you highlight the cells, then hit the autosum feature, it will add them for you. It actually inserts the '=Sum(cells)' formula for you, to save you typing it in by hand.

Another useful toolbar function is the *autosort* ᇫ↓ function, which sorts a row or column of figures in ascending order, by alpha or numerical criteria.

The *charting* 📖 function allows you to take a group of cells and quickly create a chart to make sense of a set of figures. We'll also use that function later in this chapter.

Another truly essential function of any spreadsheet program is the 'Undo' ↶ button. If you make a mistake in transcribing data, or you perform a calculation that stuffs up subsequent calculations, or if you muck up your data in any way, then always remember . . . undo is your friend!.

So, let's try a real-life example—the sort of thing that a relatively junior journalist might be expected to master.

Table 1 presents some selected figures from the Queensland Police Service, outlining the types of crimes committed against different groups of people. These figures date back to the year 2000, but are typical of the statistics that you may be handed by your editor, with the terse instruction, 'Whip me up a story out of these. Your deadline is 4.00 p.m.'

**Table I**

Victims of offences against person by sex and age, and by offence type, Queensland, 1998–99

| Age | Homicides | | Assaults | | Sexual Assaults | | Other Offences | | TOTAL |
|---|---|---|---|---|---|---|---|---|---|
| | Murder | Other | Serious | Minor | Rape | Other | Misc. | Robbery | Total |
| **Males** | | | | | | | | | |
| 0–14 | 2 | 10 | 554 | 464 | 31 | 314 | 205 | 87 | 1667 |
| 15–19 | 2 | 11 | 1139 | 501 | 17 | 94 | 179 | 248 | 2191 |
| 20–24 | 2 | 14 | 990 | 460 | 5 | 41 | 114 | 141 | 1767 |
| 25–29 | 2 | 16 | 925 | 823 | 9 | 58 | 172 | 114 | 2119 |
| 30–34 | 1 | 19 | 698 | 615 | 7 | 32 | 147 | 68 | 1587 |
| 35–39 | 4 | 18 | 602 | 475 | 7 | 10 | 136 | 74 | 1321 |
| 40–44 | 4 | 7 | 456 | 319 | 2 | 8 | 118 | 57 | 969 |
| 45–49 | 3 | 2 | 314 | 207 | 0 | 9 | 115 | 45 | 696 |
| 50–54 | 3 | 3 | 237 | 155 | 1 | 3 | 90 | 39 | 530 |
| 55 + | 5 | 7 | 276 | 181 | 0 | 4 | 101 | 87 | 661 |
| Unknown | 0 | 4 | 273 | 351 | 0 | 27 | 116 | 25 | 796 |
| **Total** | **28** | **111** | **6464** | **4551** | **72** | **600** | **1493** | **985** | **14 304** |
| **Females** | | | | | | | | | |
| 0–14 | 3 | 5 | 362 | 278 | 98 | 1018 | 190 | 12 | 1966 |
| 15–19 | 3 | 7 | 656 | 473 | 181 | 495 | 237 | 116 | 2168 |
| 20–24 | 7 | 4 | 652 | 500 | 116 | 194 | 246 | 74 | 1793 |
| 25–29 | 7 | 13 | 633 | 447 | 82 | 183 | 263 | 60 | 1688 |
| 30–34 | 2 | 4 | 414 | 256 | 59 | 108 | 182 | 41 | 1066 |
| 35–39 | 2 | 8 | 405 | 265 | 53 | 93 | 163 | 49 | 1038 |
| 40–44 | 2 | 0 | 282 | 176 | 25 | 42 | 144 | 56 | 727 |
| 45–49 | 0 | 2 | 150 | 135 | 21 | 34 | 98 | 32 | 472 |
| 50–54 | 0 | 3 | 116 | 84 | 6 | 16 | 67 | 27 | 319 |
| 55 + | 1 | 9 | 94 | 76 | 8 | 24 | 95 | 102 | 409 |
| Unknown | 1 | 1 | 130 | 113 | 8 | 95 | 108 | 9 | 465 |
| **Total** | **28** | **56** | **3894** | **2803** | **657** | **2302** | **1793** | **578** | **12 111** |
| **All People** | **56** | **167** | **10 358** | **7354** | **729** | **2902** | **3286** | **1563** | **26 415** |

**Table I**

Let's place some of those figures into a spreadsheet. We suggest you do this yourself, but in the meantime here are some screen captures.

First, type up the number of assaults by age group and gender (Figure 2).

**Figure 2**

| | A | B | C | D |
|---|---|---|---|---|
| 1 | Age | Assaults | | Total Assaults |
| 2 | Males | Serious | Minor | |
| 3 | 0-14 | 554 | 464 | |
| 4 | 15-19 | 1139 | 501 | |
| 5 | 20-24 | 990 | 460 | |
| 6 | 25-29 | 925 | 823 | |
| 7 | 30-34 | 698 | 615 | |
| 8 | 35-39 | 602 | 475 | |
| 9 | 40-44 | 456 | 319 | |
| 10 | 45-49 | 314 | 207 | |
| 11 | 50-54 | 237 | 155 | |
| 12 | 55 + | 276 | 181 | |
| 13 | Unknown | 273 | 351 | |
| 14 | Total | 6464 | 4551 | |
| 15 | Females | | | |
| 16 | 0-14 | 362 | 278 | |
| 17 | 15-19 | 656 | 473 | |
| 18 | 20-24 | 652 | 500 | |
| 19 | 25-29 | 633 | 447 | |
| 20 | 30-34 | 414 | 256 | |
| 21 | 35-39 | 405 | 265 | |
| 22 | 40-44 | 282 | 176 | |
| 23 | 45-49 | 150 | 135 | |
| 24 | 50-54 | 116 | 84 | |
| 25 | 55 + | 94 | 76 | |
| 26 | Unknown | 130 | 113 | |
| 27 | Total | 3894 | 2803 | |
| 28 | | | | |

Then we'll use the 'autosum' button to add the types of assault together (Figure 3) . . .

**Figure 3**

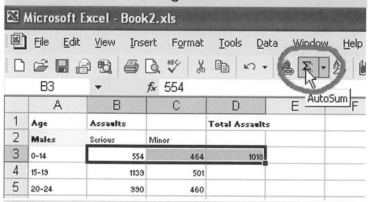

... and drag down the 'Total' column, holding on to the 'AutoFill' button in the bottom right corner of the cell (Figure 4).

**Figure 4**

| 23 | 45-49 | | 150 | 135 | 285 |
| 24 | 50-54 | | 116 | 84 | 200 |
| 25 | 55 + | | 94 | 76 | 170 |
| 26 | Unknown | | 130 | 113 | 243 |
| 27 | **Total** | | **3894** | **2803** | 6697 |
| 28 | | | | | |
| 29 | | | | | |

Then, using the autosum button, we add the total assaults against males with the total assaults against females, to get all assaults in Queensland in 1999–2000. In our case, cell D14 contains total assaults against males, and D27 all assaults against females . . . so the formula is '=D14+D27' (see Figure 5).

203

## Figure 5

| | | | | |
|---|---|---|---|---|
| 25 | 55 + | 94 | 76 | 170 |
| 26 | Unknown | 130 | 113 | 243 |
| 27 | **Total** | **3894** | **2803** | **6697** |
| 28 | | | | |
| 29 | **All Ppl** | | =D14+D27 | |
| 30 | | | | |
| 31 | | | | |

From these figures, you could show, for example, that there were 17 712 assaults reported to police, of which 170 were against women aged over 55, compared with 1749 assaults against 25–29-year-old men. So much for the 'granny-bashing epidemic' that is reported so often!

Before we go much further, it's time for a refresher in some basic mathematics—just in case you don't remember how to calculate percentages.

To determine what percentage one number is of another, you divide the number in question by the total and then multiply by 100. For example, to find out what per cent 25 is of 200, you divide 25 by 200 (0.125) then multiply by 100 to get 12.5 per cent.

Using that new-found (or newly remembered) knowledge, let's consider another story based on these figures: the sexual assault rate against young women. Again, here are some screen-shots, although I urge you to follow along on a spreadsheet of your own.

First, create a spreadsheet with demographic information, listing sexual assaults, a blank column for total sex assaults, and a separate column for total crimes. Then, using 'autosum', get a total for all sex assaults (see Figure 6).

**Hint**: *If you highlight all the sex assaults, as well as the blank column to their right, then hit autosum, Excel will fill in all the additions at the same time.*

## Figure 6

| | A | B | C | D | AutoSum |
|---|---|---|---|---|---|
| 1 | Age | Sexual Assaults | | Total Sex Assaults | Total Crimes |
| 2 | Males | Rape | Other | | |
| 3 | 0-14 | 31 | 314 | 345 | 1667 |
| 4 | 15-19 | 17 | 94 | 111 | 2191 |
| 5 | 20-24 | 5 | 41 | 46 | 1767 |
| 6 | 25-29 | 9 | 58 | 67 | 2119 |
| 7 | 30-34 | 7 | 32 | 39 | 1587 |
| 8 | 35-39 | 2 | 10 | 12 | 1321 |
| 9 | 40-44 | 0 | 8 | 8 | 969 |
| 10 | 45-49 | 1 | 9 | 10 | 636 |
| 11 | 50-54 | 0 | 3 | 3 | 530 |
| 12 | 55 + | 0 | 4 | 4 | 661 |
| 13 | Unknown | 0 | 27 | 27 | 796 |
| 14 | Total | 72 | 600 | 672 | 14304 |
| 15 | Females | | | | |
| 16 | 0-14 | 98 | 1018 | 1116 | 1966 |
| 17 | 15-19 | 181 | 495 | 676 | 2168 |
| 18 | 20-24 | 116 | 194 | 310 | 1733 |
| 19 | 25-29 | 82 | 183 | 265 | 1688 |
| 20 | 30-34 | 59 | 108 | 167 | 1066 |
| 21 | 35-39 | 53 | 93 | 146 | 1038 |
| 22 | 40-44 | 25 | 42 | 67 | 727 |
| 23 | 45-49 | 21 | 34 | 55 | 472 |
| 24 | 50-54 | 6 | 16 | 22 | 319 |
| 25 | 55 + | 8 | 24 | 32 | 409 |
| 26 | Unknown | 8 | 95 | 103 | 465 |
| 27 | Total | 657 | 2302 | 2959 | 12111 |
| 28 | | | | | |

Now we are going to check out what percentage of crimes against people are sex crimes. Create a new column marked 'Sex Assault %'. Click on the letter for that column (in our case, column F) (see Figure 7).

## Figure 7

| | A | B | C | D | E | F |
|---|---|---|---|---|---|---|
| | | | fx Sex Assault % | | | |
| 1 | Age | Sexual Assaults | | Total Sex Assaults | Total Crimes | Sex Assault % |
| 2 | Males | Rape | Other | | | |
| 3 | 0-14 | 31 | 314 | 345 | 1667 | |
| 4 | 15-19 | 17 | 94 | 111 | 2191 | |

When that column is highlighted, choose the format menu, then 'cells', then 'percentages', then 1 decimal place (see Figure 8).

**Figure 8**

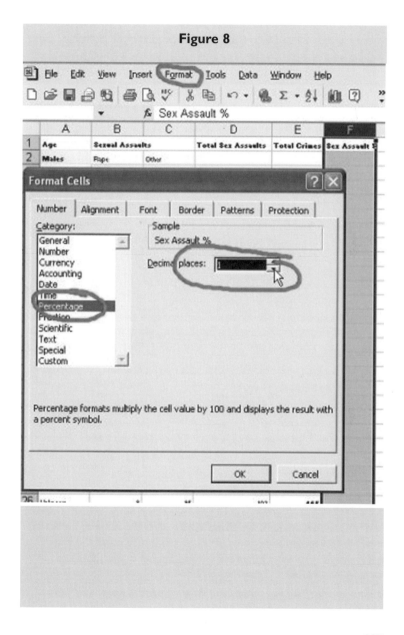

Then calculate the percentages by dividing the number of sex crimes by the number of all crimes. Use the formula 'Total Sex Assaults/Total Crimes'. In our case, that means entering the formula '=D3/E3' into cell F3, and then using the 'fill down' handle to fill in the rest of the results in column F (see Figure 9).

**Figure 9**

| | F3 | ▼ | fx =D3/E3 | Formula Bar | | |
|---|---|---|---|---|---|---|
| | A | B | C | | E | F |
| 1 | Age | Sexual Assaults | | Total Sex Assaults | Total Crimes | Sex Assault % |
| 2 | Males | Rape | Other | | | |
| 3 | 0-14 | 31 | 314 | 345 | 1667 | 20.7% |
| 4 | 15-19 | 17 | 94 | 111 | 2191 | 5.1% |
| 5 | 20-24 | 5 | 41 | 46 | 1767 | 2.6% |
| 6 | 25-29 | 9 | 58 | 67 | 2119 | 3.2% |
| 7 | 30-34 | 7 | 32 | 39 | 1587 | 2.5% |
| 8 | 35-39 | 2 | 10 | 12 | 1321 | 0.9% |
| 9 | 40-44 | 0 | 8 | 8 | 969 | 0.8% |
| 10 | 45-49 | 1 | 9 | 10 | 696 | 1.4% |
| 11 | 50-54 | 0 | 3 | 3 | 530 | 0.6% |
| 12 | 55+ | 0 | 4 | 4 | 661 | 0.6% |
| 13 | Unknown | 0 | 27 | 27 | 796 | 3.4% |
| 14 | Total | 72 | 600 | 672 | 14304 | 4.7% |
| 15 | Females | | | | | |
| 16 | 0-14 | 98 | 1018 | 1116 | 1966 | 56.8% |
| 17 | 15-19 | 181 | 495 | 676 | 2168 | 31.2% |
| 18 | 20-24 | 116 | 194 | 310 | 1793 | 17.3% |
| 19 | 25-29 | 82 | 183 | 265 | 1688 | 15.7% |
| 20 | 30-34 | 59 | 108 | 167 | 1066 | 15.7% |
| 21 | 35-39 | 53 | 93 | 146 | 1038 | 14.1% |
| 22 | 40-44 | 25 | 42 | 67 | 727 | 9.2% |
| 23 | 45-49 | 21 | 34 | 55 | 472 | 11.7% |
| 24 | 50-54 | 6 | 16 | 22 | 319 | 6.9% |
| 25 | 55+ | 8 | 24 | 32 | 409 | 7.8% |
| 26 | Unknown | 8 | 95 | 103 | 465 | 22.2% |
| 27 | Total | 657 | 2302 | 2959 | 12111 | 24.4% |

This will show you that, for example, nearly 57 per cent of all crimes against pre-teen and younger teenage girls are sexual assaults—and nearly 21 per cent of all crimes against younger boys are of a similar nature.

Now, it's time to use Excel's *charting* function to create some simple charts to go with the news stories that you have extracted from these figures. The first will show the level of crime, both sexual and other, against each age group of women. Begin by copying the 'Female' section from your existing spreadsheet (see Figure 10). Don't worry about the '%' column or the total at the base of each column: you won't need them.

# Figure 10

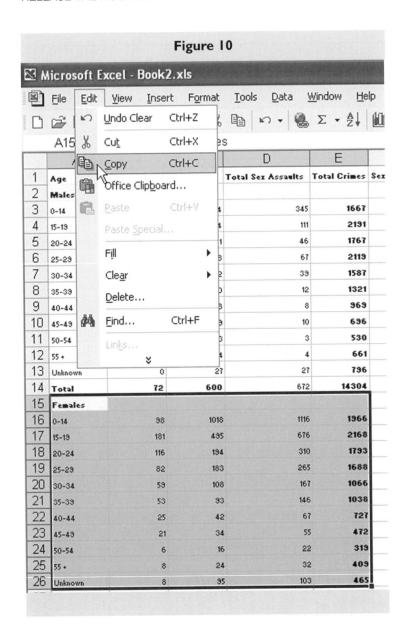

Then, paste the data anywhere else on your work-sheet, using the 'paste special'—values command (see Figure 11). If 'paste special' does not appear on your 'edit' menu, click on the 'more' button, also under the 'edit' menu.

**Figure 11**

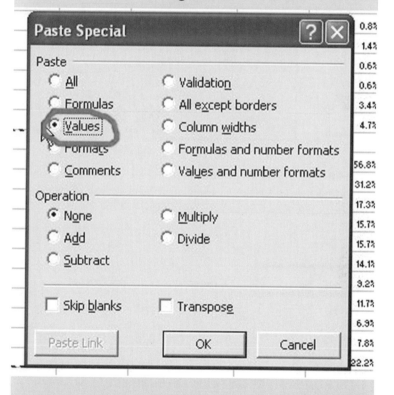

Delete the first two columns of figures. These are 'Rape' and 'Other' figures, but we only need the totals (see Figure 12).

**Figure 12**

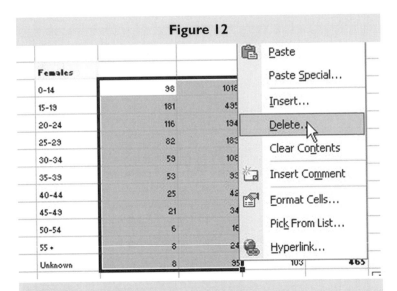

On the top row of your figures, delete the 'Female' heading, and add 'Sex Crimes' and 'All Crimes' above the second and third columns (see Figure 13)

**Figure 13**

| | Sex Crimes | All Crimes |
|---|---|---|
| 0–14 | 1116 | **1966** |
| 15–19 | 676 | **2168** |
| 20–24 | 310 | **1793** |

Now, highlight everything in your new data set and hit the Chart button (or use 'chart' from the 'insert' menu) (see Figure 14).

**Figure 14**

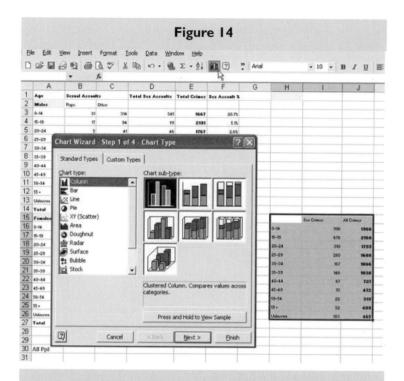

First, you are going to create a 'Column' chart which shows how girls and young women are more likely to be victims of all crimes, but particularly of sex-related crimes. Then you'll create a pie-chart which shows, quite starkly, how two-thirds of all sex crimes are perpetrated against girls and teenagers.

Using the chart-wizard, as just outlined, click on 'column type', and choose the final option, '3D Column' (see Figure 15).

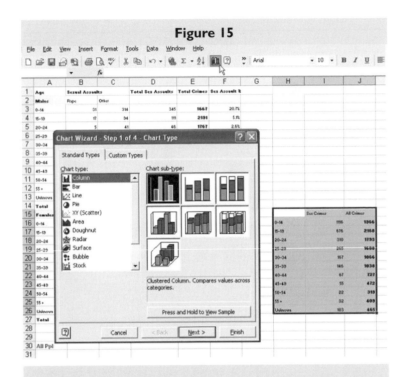

Figure 15

Simply click 'finish', and then click anywhere in the chart box which is created. Click your *right* mouse button, select 'chart options', and under 'chart title' put a title of your choice (see Figure 16).

**Figure 16**

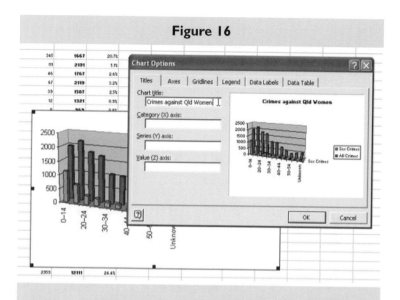

Finally, create a pie-chart using the figures you extracted before.

Go back to your Excel worksheet, and if necessary move the chart you created out of the way. Select just the first two columns—the one with ages, and the one headed 'Sex Crimes'. Using the 'chart' tool, choose 'exploded pie'. Again, choose 'finish' (see Figure 17).

**Figure 17**

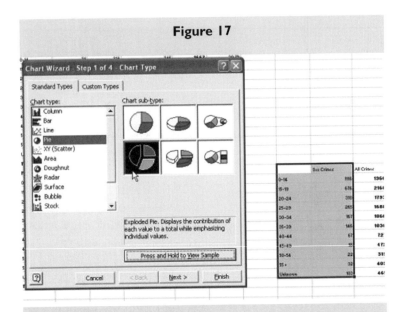

Click on the chart frame, right-click and select 'chart options', then name the chart. You might also like to choose a different location for the legend (see Figure 18).

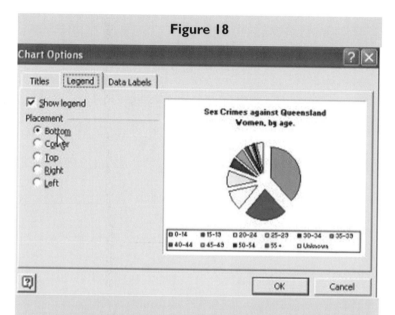

**Figure 18**

Of course, whether you use a spreadsheet to create a chart, to determine percentages, to highlight trends, or to confirm suspicions, you should always remember the most famous of computer acronyms: GIGO— Garbage In, Garbage Out.

If you make an error entering the data in a spreadsheet, or if the data itself is flawed, then the conclusions that you draw will also be flawed. You must always 'interrogate the data' and ensure that you are drawing the right conclusions. Again, if the results you are getting seem too good to be true, they probably are.

But even if the figures are accurate, you also need to place a 'human face' on the data that you extract, because numbers are, in and of themselves, pretty boring. There's nothing quite as snore-inducing as dry, dull and dusty data . . . but if those figures can be 'fleshed out' and given form, then you have the makings of a good story.

As I said at the beginning of this section, a spreadsheet won't write your story for you. But, used intelligently, it can help you ask the sorts of questions that will make your story *almost* write itself.

And that's the sort of help that *all* working journos can use.

# APPENDIX

## WHO HAS WHAT? RESOURCES UNDER SUBJECT TOPICS

This section contains a brief list of recommended resources, under broad topics that are often researched by journalists and writers.

These resources are listed under the same categories of sources of information as have been described previously. Rather than a comprehensive list of resources, these lists amount to a brief sniff around these areas to scout out some interesting possibilities. Add to them to make your own collection!

### Arts/Films/Music

**Archives**

Archives (Electronic Australiana—NLA): www.nla.gov.au/oz/#arch

Directory of Archives in Australia: www.archivists.org.au/directory/asa_dir.htm

Register of Australian Archives and Manuscripts: www.nla.gov.au/raam

**Businesses**

Commonwealth Securities Ltd: www.comsec.com.au

**Community, culture, events**

Adelaide Festival of Arts: www.adelaidefestival.org.au

AusStage—Gateway to the Australian Performing Arts: www.ausstage.edu.au

**Databases, directories, search engines**

AcqWeb's Directory of Book Reviews: http://acqweb.library.vanderbilt.edu

Amazon Books: www.amazon.com
Artfiles: www.artfiles.com.au
Australia Dancing:
 www.australiadancing.org
Australian Visual Arts Database
 (AVAD), Discovery Media,
 Sydney, 1999–
BookWire: www.bookwire.com
First Look:
 www.firstlook.movie.new.net
The Internet Movie Database:
 www.imdb.com
Ozlit:
 http://home.vicnet.net.au/~ozlit

**Friends and foes**
Ain't it cool news:
 www.aint-it-cool-news.com

**Government agencies**
Arts Queensland:
 www.arts.qld.gov.au
Australia Council for the Arts:
 www.ozco.gov.au
Australian Office of Film and
 Literature Classification:
 www.oflc.gov.au
Culture and recreation portal: www.
 cultureandrecreation.gov.au
Department of Communications,
 Information Technology and the
 Arts (Australia):
 www.dcita.gov.au

**Indexes and databases**
*Art Index*, H.W. Wilson, Bronx NY,
 1995–
*AustLIT: the Australian Literary
 Database*, RMIT Publishing,
 Melbourne, 1988–
*Design And Applied Arts Index
 (DAAI)*, Design Documentation,
 Etchingham UK, 1987–
*Gale's Literary Index*:
 www.galenet.com/servlet/
 LitIndex

**Legal**
Austlii: www.austlii.edu.au
Legislation—Arts and Culture
 (DCITA):
 www.dcita.gov.au/arts/legislation
WebLaw: www.WebLaw.edu.au

**Libraries**
Australian Libraries Gateway:
 www.nla.gov.au/apps/libraries
ANU Institute of the Arts Library
 & Resource Centre:
 www.anu.edu.au/ITA/AusArts/

**News reports**
ABC's Online Arts Gateway
 newsletter:
 http://abc.net.au/arts/mail.htm
Arts and Letters Daily:
 www.cybereditions.com/aldaily

**Online communities**
Ozlists: www.gu.edu.au/ozlists

**Organisations**
ABC Arts Online:
 www.abc.net.au/arts
The Arts Law Centre:
 www.artslaw.com.au
The Australian Dance Council:
 www.ausdance.org.au
Australian Museums and Galleries
 On Line (AMOL):
 http://amol.org.au
Music Australia:
 www.musicaustralia.org
National Gallery of Australia:
 www.nga.gov.au/Home/
 index.cfm
Regional Arts Australia:
 www.regionalarts.com.au

**Periodicals**
*Artbeat*: www.dcita.gov.au/arts/
 publications/artbeat

*Australian Humanities Review*:
www.lib.latrobe.edu.au/AHR
*FineArt Forum*:
www.fineartforum.org
*State of the Arts*:
www.stateart.com.au/sota/

### Politicians, parliament

Parliament of Australia—Who's
Who: www.aph.gov.au/
whoswho/index.htm

### Press releases

Newsroom, Department of
Communications, Information
Technology and the Arts:
www.dcita.gov.au/newsroom
Press Release Centre:
www.pressrelease.com.au

### Reference

Art Almanac: www.art-
almanac.com.au
*Book Review Index*, Gale Research
Co., Detroit MI, 1965–
McCulloch, A. Rev. and updated
by McCulloch, S. 1994, *The
Encyclopaedia of Australian Art*,
3rd edn, Allen & Unwin,
Sydney
*The New Grove Dictionary of Music
and Musicians,* Oxford
University Press, Oxford, 1999–

### Statistics

Australian Statistics on the
Internet (NLA):
www.nla.gov.au/oz/stats.html

### Universities, research
### institutes

Creative Industries Research and
Applications Centre (CIRAC),
QUT:
www.creativeindustries.qut.com/
research/cirac/index.jsp

## Business

### Archives

Directory of Archives in Australia:
www.archivists.org.au/directory/
asa_dir.htm
Guide to Australian Business
Records: www.archivists.org.
au/busrec/index.html
Register of Australian Archives and
Manuscripts (RAAM):
www.nla.gov.au/raam

### Businesses

*The Annual Report Collection,*
Connect 4, Melbourne, 1993–
Annual report gallery:
www.reportgallery.com
Commonwealth Securities Ltd:
www.comsec.com.au
Datamonitor:
www.datamonitor.com
MarketResearch.com:
www.marketresearch.com
NZX: www.nzse.co.nz
Oz Forex Foreign Exchange:
www.ozforex.com.au
Stock Exchanges of the World:
www.internationalist.com/
business/stocks
Sydney Futures Exchange:
www.sfe.com.au

### Community, culture, events

Australian Institute of
Management—Management
Excellence Awards: www.
managementawards.com.au
Conference of Major
Superannuation Funds:
www.cmsf.com.au

### Databases, directories,
### search engines

a'Court's Business Handbook:
www.acourt.co.nz

Australian Securities and Investment Commission (ASIC): www.asic.gov.au

Australian Stock Exchange: www.asx.com.au/asx

Bloomberg L.P.: www.bloomberg.com

*The Business Who's Who of Australia*: http://bww.dnb.com.au/default.asp

CITEC Confirm: www.confirm.com.au

Commonwealth Securities Ltd: www.comsec.com.au

Connect4: www.connect4.com.au

*FinAnalysis*, Aspect Financial, Sydney, 1990–

IP Australia Patents: www.ipaustralia.gov.au/patents/search_index.shtml

Kompass Australia, Kompass New Zealand: www.kompass.com

New Zealand *Yellow Pages*: www.yellowpages.co.nz

Shareinfo: www.shareinfo.co.nz

Yahoo! Australia and NZ Finance: http://au.finance.yahoo.com

## Friends and foes

CorpWatch: www.corpwatch.org

## Government agencies

AusIndustry, Australian Commonwealth Government: www.ausindustry.gov.au

Australian Business Register: www.abr.gov.au/ABR_BC/

Australian Competition and Consumer Commission: www.accc.gov.au

Australian Prudential Regulation Authority (APRA): www.apra.gov.au

Australian Securities and Investment Commission: www.asic.gov.au

Business Entry Point: www.business.gov.au

Business Information Zone New Zealand: www.biz.org.nz

Consumer.gov.au: www.consumer.gov.au

Insolvency and Trustee Service Australia (ITSA): www.itsa.gov.au

Intellectual Property Office of New Zealand: www.iponz.govt.nz/search/cad/dbssiten.main

IP Australia (Australian trademarks and patents): www.ipaustralia.gov.au

New Zealand Companies Office: www.companies.govt.nz/search/cad/dbssiten.main

New Zealand Trade and Enterprise: www.industrynz.govt.nz

New Zealand Treasury: www.treasury.govt.nz

Personal Property Securities Register (New Zealand): www.ppsr.govt.nz

Productivity Commission: www.pc.gov.au

Reserve Bank of Australia: www.rba.gov.au

## Indexes and databases

*ABI/Inform Global*, UMI, Ann Arbor MI, 1971–

*Australasian Business Intelligence* (ABIX): www.abix.com.au

*Australian Public Affairs—Full Text* (APA-FT), RMIT Publishing, Melbourne, 1995–

*Business Source Premier*, Ebsco, Birmingham AL, 1990–

*Aspect Dat Analysis*, Aspect Financial, Sydney 1990–

*Factiva*, Dow Jones Reuters Business Interactive (US), 1985–

News Store—Fairfax publications: http://newsstore.f2.com.au/apps/newsSearch.ac

Newstext: www.newstext.com.au

### Legal

Austlii: www.austlii.edu.au

### Libraries

Australian Broadcasting Authority library: www.aba.gov.au/aba/library/index.htm

Australian Libraries Gateway—Library type—'Corporate/Business': www.nla.gov.au/apps/libraries

### News reports

Australian Broadcasting Corporation: www.abc.net.au

*Australian Financial Review*: http://afr.com

*Business Daily Review*: www.businessdailyreview.com

*Financial Times Asia*: http://news.ft.com/home/asia

*Trademark*: www.austrade.gov.au

Yahoo! Australia & NZ News—Business: http://au.news.yahoo.com/business

### Online communities

Business Weblogs (Yahoo! Directory): http://dir.yahoo.com/Computers_and_Internet/Internet/World_Wide_Web/Weblogs/Business/

### Organisations

Agribusiness New Zealand: www.agribusinessnz.org.nz

Australian Chamber of Commerce and Industry: www.acci.asn.au

Australian Council of Trade Unions: www.actu.asn.au

Australian Institute of Company Directors: www.companydirectors.com.au

Australian Shareholders' Association: www.asa.asn.au

Business Council of Australia: www.bca.com.au

International Monetary Fund (IMF): www.imf.org

New Zealand Chambers of Commerce and Industry: www.nzchambers.co.nz

New Zealand Council of Trade Unions (CTU): www.union.org.nz

World Bank: www.worldbank.org

### Periodicals

*Australian Business and Investment Explorer* (ABIE), Business Explorer Press, Sydney, 2002–

*Australian Business Monthly* (ABM), Australian Consolidated Press, Sydney, 1991–

*Asia-Pacific Journal of Economics and Business*, IRIC, Perth, 1997–

*Business Review Weekly* (BRW): www.brw.com.au

Crikey.com: www.crikey.com.au

*The Economist*: www.economist.com

*The Independent*: www.theindependent.co.nz/index.html

*University of Auckland Business Review*: www.uabr.auckland.ac.nz

## Politicians, parliament
Parliament of Australia—Who's
Who: www.aph.gov.au/
whoswho/index.htm

## Press releases
Business Wire:
www.businesswire.com
News and Events—New Zealand
Trade and Enterprise:
www.nzte.govt.nz
Press Release Centre:
www.pressrelease.com.au

## Reference
Glossary of sharemarket terms:
www.asx.com.au/webmcq/servlet/
com.webmcq.glossary.Glossary?
cid=0&alt=1
*International Business Rankings*,
Express Information, State
Library of Victoria, Melbourne,
2003–
InvestorWords dictionary:
www.investorwords.com
International Monetary Fund
(IMF) World Economic Outlook
Reports: www.
imf.org/external/pubs/ft/weo

## Statistics
Australian Bureau of Statistics:
www.abs.gov.au
Statistical Data Locators (Nanyang
Technological University):
www.ntu.edu.sg/lib/stat/statdata.
htm
Statistics New Zealand—Te Tari
Tatau: www.stats.govt.nz

## Universities, research institutes
Australian universities (Australian
Vice Chancellors' Committee):
www.avcc.edu.au
Centre for Corporate Law and

Securities Regulation, University
of Melbourne:
http://cclsr.law.unimelb.edu.au
Committee for Economic
Development of Australia:
www.ceda.com.au/New/Flash/
index.html
Queensland International Business
Research Concentration (QUT):
www.bus.qut.edu.au/schools/int
ernational/research/qibrc.jsp

# Education
## Archives
Archives (Electronic Australiana—
NLA): www.nla.gov.au/oz/#arch
Directory of Archives in Australia:
www.archivists.org.au/directory/
asa_dir.htm
Register of Australian Archives
and Manuscripts:
www.nla.gov.au/raam

## Businesses
Commonwealth Securities Ltd:
www.comsec.com.au

## Community, culture, events
Education Network Australia
(EdNA): www.edna.edu.au/edna/
page1.html
School term dates: www.
dest.gov.au/schools/dates.htm

## Databases, directories, search engines
EdNA Online: www.edna.edu.au/
edna.page1.html
Research Resources for the Social
Sciences: www.socsciresearch.com
The Scout Report: www.
scout.cs.wisc.edu/scout/report

## Friends and foes
Australian universities (Australian
Vice-Chancellors' Committee):
www.avcc.edu.au/

Online Opinion:
www.onlineopinion.com.au
State departments of education
(*OzGuide*):
http://journoz.com/educ.html

## Government agencies

Australian Research Council
(ARC): www.arc.gov.au
Department of Education,
Science and Training (DEST)
(Australia): www.dest.gov.au
New Zealand Ministry of
Education:
www.minedu.govt.nz

## Indexes and databases

*Australian Education Index* (AEI),
Informit, Melbourne, 1978–
*ProQuest Education Journals*, UMI,
Ann Arbor MI, 1988–

## Legal

Austlii: www.austlii.edu.au

## Libraries

Australian Libraries Gateway:
www.nla.gov.au/apps/libraries
Department of Education Library
and Information Centre—
Tasmania: www.education.
tas.gov.au/delic

## News reports

*Campus Review*:
www.camrev.com.au
*Chronicle of Higher Education*:
www.chronicle.com
*NewsTrawler*:
www.newstrawler.com
*The Times Higher Education
Supplement*: www.thes.co.uk

## Online communities

Ozlists—Education:
www.gu.edu.au/ozlists

## Organisations

Association of University Staff
(New Zealand): www.aus.ac.nz
Independent Schools Council of
Australia: www.ncisa.edu.au
NTEU (Australia's Union for
Tertiary Education Staff):
www.nteu.org.au/home

## Periodicals

*Issues in Educational Research*:
http://education.curtin.edu.
au/iier

## Politicians, parliament

Parliament of Australia—
Who's Who: www.aph.gov.au/
whoswho/index.htm

## Press releases

EDNA Online media releases:
www.edna.edu.au/edna/go/pid/
336
News (Australian Vice Chancellors'
Committee): www.avcc.edu.au
Press Release Centre:
www.pressrelease.com.au

## Reference

*Discover Australian university
handbooks*:
www.nla.gov.au/guides/discover
guides/unihandbooks.html
*The Penguin Macquarie Dictionary
of Australian Education*
Penguin in association with
Macquarie Library, Ringwood,
Victoria, 1989

## Statistics

Australian Statistics on the Internet
(NLA):
www.nla.gov.au/oz/stats.html
University Statistics Director,
Department of Education,
Science and Training:
www.dest.gov.au

## Universities, research institutes

Australian Council of Education Research: www.acer.edu.au

New Zealand universities (Te Puna Web Directory): http://webdirectory.natlib.govt.nz/dir/en/nz/education/tertiary-education/universities/

# Environment, agriculture

**Archives**

Archives (Electronic Australiana—NLA): www.nla.gov.au/oz/#arch

Directory of Archives in Australia: www.archivists.org.au/directory/asa_dir.htm

Register of Australian Archives and Manuscripts: www.nla.gov.au/raam

**Businesses**

American Petroleum Institute: www.api.org

Australian Environment Industry Directory: www.wme.com.au/aeid

Oil and Gas Online: www.oilandgasonline.com

**Community, culture, events**

National Toxics Network Inc. Australia: www.oztoxics.org/ntn/index.html

**Databases, directories, search engines**

EcoPortal: www.eco-portal.com

The Environmental Directory: www.webdirectory.com

Food and Agriculture Organisation Statistical Databases (FAOSTAT): http://apps.fao.org/

*Green Pages* (New Zealand): www.greenpages.org.nz

GreenNet: www.gn.apc.org/index.shtml

National Pollutant Inventory: www.npi.gov.au

World Directory of Environment Organisations: www.interenvironment.org/wd/index.htm

**Friends and foes**

Rainforest Action Network: www.ran.org

**Government agencies**

Australian Department of the Environment and Heritage: www.deh.gov.au/index.html

CSIRO Australia: www.csiro.au/csiro.html

Department of Environment (WA): www.environment.wa.gov.au

Energy Information Administration: www.eia.doe.gov

NSW Government Portal—Environment: www.nsw.gov.au/environment.asp

Organisation of the Petroleum Exporting Countries (OPEC): www.opec.org

**Indexes and databases**

*AGRICOLA—AGRICultural OnLine Access*: http://agricola.nal.usda.gov

*REEF—Great Barrier Reef Marine Park Database*, RMIT Publishing, Melbourne, 1982–

**Legal**

Austlii: www.austlii.edu.au

Environmental law—University of Adelaide: www.law.adelaide.edu.au/library/research/envlaw

**Libraries**

Australian Conservation Foundation library—Melbourne: www.acfonline.org.au

Conservation Council of South
Australia library:
www.ccsa.asn.au

The Total Environment Centre
library: www.tec.nccnsw.org.au

## News reports

Environmental News Network
(ENN): www.enn.com

Planet Ark: www.planetark.org

## Online communities

Envirolink Forum:
www.envirolink.org/forum/

Ozlists—Environment:
www.gu.edu.au/ozlists

## Organisations

American Council for an Energy-
Efficient Economy:
www.aceee.org

Australian Conservation
Foundation (ACF):
www.acfonline.org.au

Christchurch Environment Centre
(New Zealand):
www.environment.org.nz

Greenpeace Australia Pacific:
www.greenpeace.org.au

Mineral Policy Institute:
www.mpi.org.au

The Right-to-Know Network:
www.rtk.net

Society of Environmental
Journalists: www.sej.org

United Nations Environmental
Programme (UNEP):
www.unep.org

The World Wildlife Fund:
www.panda.org/home.htm and
www.worldwildlife.org

## Periodicals

*Issues Magazine:*
http://issues.control.com.au/
index.shtml

*Waste Management and
Environment*: www.wme.com.au/

## Politicians, parliament

Parliament of Australia—
Who's Who: www.
aph.gov.au/whoswho/index.htm

## Press releases

Press Release Centre:
www.pressrelease.com.au

## Reference

Directory of Organisations
and Institutes Active in
Environmental Monitoring:
www.gsf.de/UNEP/contents.html

## Statistics

Australian Statistical Internet
Sites (NLA):
www.nla.gov.au/oz/stats.html

Population, Demography and
Statistics (University of Sydney):
www.library.usyd.edu.au/subject
s/readyref/population.html

## Universities, research
institutes

AGRIGATE—An Agriculture
Information Gateway for
Australian Researchers:

Cooperative Research Centre for
Freshwater Ecology (University
of Canberra):
http://freshwater.canberra.edu.
au/www.agrigate.edu.au

# Food and wine

## Archives

Archives (Electronic Australiana—
NLA): www.nla.gov.au/oz/#arch

Culinary Archives and Museum,
Johnson & Wales University:
www.culinary.org

Directory of Archives in Australia: www.archivists.org.au/directory/asa_dir.htm

Register of Australian Archives and Manuscripts: www.nla.gov.au/raam

## Businesses

The Business Channel: http://business.channel.vic.gov.au

Kompass Australia, Kompass New Zealand: www.kompass.com

Le Cordon Bleu: www.cordonbleu.edu/flashindex.html

## Community, culture, events

Australian Food News—Calendar of Food Events: www.ausfoodnews.com.au

Fine Food Australia—Events: www.foodaustralia.com.au/food/events.asp

Tasting Australia: www.tasting-australia.com.au

What's on in the Food Industry: www.foodscience.afisc.csiro.au

## Databases, directories, search engines

Directory of Dining Directories: www.epicurean-kitchen.com.au/links/ Dining/ Directories

New Zealand Wine: www.nzwine.com

## Friends and foes

Australian Food and Wine website: www.campionandcurtis.com

Australian Symposium of Gastronomy, PO Box 221, Petersham NSW 2049

Gourmand International: www.internationalcookbookrevue.com

## Government agencies

Department of Agriculture, Fisheries and Forestry (Australia): www.affa.gov.au

Food Standards Australia, New Zealand: www.foodstandards.gov.au

## Indexes and databases

*Australian Public Affairs—Full Text* (APA-FT), RMIT Publishing, Melbourne, 1995–

*Expanded Academic ASAP*, Information Access Co., Foster City CA, 1980–

## Legal

Austlii: www.austlii.edu.au

Food Law and Policy Australia: www.ausfoodnews.com.au/flapa

## Politicians, parliament

Parliament of Australia—Who's Who: www.aph.gov.au/whoswho/index.htm

## Libraries

Australian Libraries Gateway: www.nla.gov.au/apps/libraries

Crop and Food Research Library (Te Puna Web Directory): http://webdirectory.natlib.govt.nz/index.htm

## News reports

Factual: the food page, BBC Radio 4: www.bbc.co.uk/radio4/factual/foodprogramme.shtml

*Good Living* section, *Sydney Morning Herald,* Charles Kemp and John Fairfax, Sydney, 1842–

## Online communities

Ozlists: www.gu.edu.au/ozlists

## Organisations

Australian Food and Grocery Council: www.afgc.org.au

Slow Food: www.slowfood.com

## Periodicals
Food Australia:
www.foodaust.com.au
Winestate: www.winestate.com.au

## Politicians, parliament
Parliament of Australia—Who's
Who: www.aph.gov.au/
whoswho/index.htm

## Press releases
Press Release Centre:
www.pressrelease.com.au

## Reference
Ayto, J. 2002, *An A to Z of Food
and Drink*, Oxford University
Press, Oxford, New York
*Culinary French: A Glossary*: www.
hvinet.com/gallen/gloss.html
*Encyclopedia of Food and Culture*,
c. 2003 Scribner, New York
Millotone, E. and Lang, T. 2003,
*Atlas of Food: Who Eats What,
Where and Why*, Earthscan,
London

## Statistics
Australian Statistical Internet Sites
(NLA):
www.nla.gov.au/oz/stats.html

## Universities, research institutes
Graduate Program in Gastronomy,
University of Adelaide:
www.adelaide.edu.au/humss/
gastronomy
Research Centre for the History of
Food and Drink, University of
Adelaide: www.arts.adelaide.
edu.au/centrefooddrink
Research Institute for the Culture
and History of Food and Drink,
Carleton University, Canada:
www.carleton.ca

# Health, medical

## Archives
Archives (Electronic Australiana—
NLA): www.nla.gov.au/oz/#arch
Directory of Archives in Australia:
www.archivists.org.au/directory/
asa_dir.htm
Register of Australian Archives and
Manuscripts:
www.nla.gov.au/raam

## Businesses
Commonwealth Securities Ltd:
www.comsec.com.au

## Community, culture, events
Calendar of Events (Department of
Health and Ageing, Australia):
www.health.gov.au
Congress Resource Center:
www.docguide.com/crc.nsf/
web-bySpec

## Databases, directories, search engines
*Australian Occupational Health and
Safety Online*, IHS Australia,
Sydney, c. 1997–
*Drug*, Informit in association with
the National Library of
Australia, Melbourne, 1974–

## Friends and foes
New South Wales Health resources:
www.health.nsw.gov.au

## Government agencies
Better Health Channel:
www.betterhealth.vic.gov.au
Centers for Disease Control and
Prevention (USA):
www.cdc.gov/ncidod
Communicable Diseases Australia:
www.health.gov.au/internet/
wcms/Publishing.nsf/Content/
Communicable+Diseases+
Australia–1

Department of Health and Ageing
(Australia): www.health.gov.au
HealthInsite:
www.healthinsite.gov.au
National Health Information
Center USA: www.health.gov
US Food and Drug Administration:
www.fda.gov
World Health Organisation
(WHO): www.who.int/en

**Indexes and databases**
*Australasian Medical Index* (AMI),
Informit, Melbourne, 1968–
*Medline*, National Library of
Medicine, New York, 1966–

**Legal**
Austlii: www.austlii.edu.au

**Libraries**
Australian Libraries Gateway—
Library type—'Health/Medical':
www.nla.gov.au/apps/libraries
Cochrane Library:
www.thecochranelibrary.com
Family Planning Association
library, 70 Rose Street,
Perth WA 6000, Australia
US National Library of Medicine:
www.nlm.nih.gov/nlmhome.html

**News reports**
Health Matters Library (ABC):
www.abc.net.au/health/library
Health News UK: www.health-
news.co.uk

**Online communities**
Ozlists—Medical and Health:
www.gu.edu.au/ozlists

**Organisations**
Australian Medical Association
(AMA): www.ama.com.au
Children by Choice:
www.childrenbychoice.org.au

Organising Medical Networked
Information: http://omni.ac.uk
World Health Organisation
(WHO): www.who.int

**Periodicals**
*Australian Doctor*:
www.australiandoctor.com.au
*The British Medical Journal*:
http://bmj.bmjjournals.com
*The Lancet*: www.thelancet.com
*The Medical Journal of Australia*:
www.mja.com.au
*The New England Journal of
Medicine* (US):
http://content.nejm.org/
*Nursing Times*:
www.nursingtimes.net

**Politicians, parliament**
Parliament of Australia—
Who's Who: www.aph.gov.au/
whoswho/index.htm

**Press releases**
Press Release Centre:
www.pressrelease.com.au

**Reference**
*Black's Medical Dictionary*, 40th
edn, A & C Black, London,
c. 2002
Merck Medical Manuals:
www.merck.com/pubs
On-line Medical Dictionary:
http://cancerweb.ncl.ac.uk/omd

**Statistics**
Australian Institute of Health and
Welfare resources:
www.aihw.gov.au
Australian Statistical Internet Sites
(NLA):
www.nla.gov.au/oz/stats.html
*Australia's Young People: Their
Health and Wellbeing,*

Australian Institute of Health and Welfare, Canberra, 1991–

Public Health Information Development Unit (PHIDU): www.publichealth.gov.au

WHO Statistical Information System (WHOSIS): www3.who.int/whosis/menu.cfm

## Universities, research institutes

Australian Centre for Youth Studies: www.acys.utas.edu. au/ncys/topics/drugs.htm

Australian universities (Australian Vice-Chancellors' Committee): www.avcc.edu.au

The Garvan Institute: www.garvan.org.au

International Agency for Research on Cancer: www.iarc.fr

Menzies School of Health Research: www.menzies.edu.au

# Peace, security

## Archives

Archives (Electronic Australiana—NLA): www.nla.gov.au/oz/#arch

Directory of Archives in Australia: www.archivists.org.au/directory/asa_dir.htm

National Security Archive: www.gwu.edu/~nsarchiv/NSAEBB/NSAEBB55/index1.html

Register of Australian Archives and Manuscripts: www.nla.gov.au/raam

## Businesses

Australian Export—Australian Trade Commission: www.austrade.gov.au

## Community, culture, events

United Nations Conferences and Events: www.un.org/events

## Databases, directories, search engines

*Asian resources: A select directory of databases (ASIANRES)*, RMIT Publishing, Melbourne, 1996–

*Columbia International Affairs Online* (CIAO), Columbia University Press, New York, 1997–

International Relations and Security Network: www.isn.ethz.ch/index.cfm

NIRA's World Directory of Think Tanks: www.nira.go.jp

## Friends and foes

Strategic and Defence Studies Centre: http://rspas.anu.edu.au/sdsc

Terrorism Knowledge Base: www.tkb.org

ZNet's Chomsky Archive: www.zmag.org/chomsky/index.cfm

## Government agencies

Department of Foreign Affairs and Trade (Australia): www.dfat.gov.au

Defence Intelligence Organisation (DIO): www.defence.gov.au/dio

Ministry of Defence, New Zealand: www.defence.govt.nz

Ministry of Defence, United Kingdom: www.mod.uk

National Security Council: www.whitehouse.gov/nsc

## Indexes and databases

*Expanded Academic ASAP*, Information Access, Foster City CA, 1998–

*Intan Mas: Indonesian and Southeast Asia*, Informit, Melbourne, 1989–

*PAIS International*, Ovid
  Technologies, New York, 1972–

## Legal
Austlii: www.austlii.edu.au
WebLaw: www.WebLaw.edu.au

## Libraries
Australian Libraries Gateway—
  Library type—'Defence/Military':
  www.nla.gov.au/apps/libraries

## News reports
The Coombsweb:
  http://coombs.anu.edu.au
*Dialog Global Reporter*, Dialog,
  Cary NC, 1997–
Go Asia Pacific—ABC Gateway to
  Asia Pacific:
  www.goasiapacific.com

## Online communities
Ozlists: www.gu.edu.au/ozlists

## Organisations
Arms Sales Monitoring Project:
  www.fas.org/asmp
Australian Strategic Policy
  Institute: www.aspi.org.au
Centre for Nonproliferation
  Databases: http://cns.miis.edu
Migration Information Source:
  www.migrationinformation.org
North Atlantic Treaty Organisation
  (NATO):
  www.nato.int/home.htm
Project Ploughshares:
  www.ploughshares.ca
South Asia Terrorism:
  www.satp.org/default.asp
United Nations: www.un.org

## Periodicals
The Diplomat Online: www.
  the-diplomat.com

## Politicians, parliament
Parliament of Australia—
  Who's Who: www.aph.gov.au/
  whoswho/index.htm

## Press releases
*Defence News Online*:
  www.defence.gov.au/news
Press Release Centre:
  www.pressrelease.com.au
Press releases, Minister for
  Defence, New Zealand (through
  Portfolios—Defence):
  www.beehive.govt.nz/

## Reference
Bolz, F., c. 2002, *The
  Counterterrorism Handbook:
  Tactics, Procedures, and
  Techniques*, CRC Press, Boca
  Raton FL
*Directory of Australian Associations*,
  Information Australia,
  Melbourne, 1978–
*Encyclopedia of Violence, Peace
  and Conflict*, Academic Press,
  San Diego, Sydney,
  c. 1999

## Statistics
Australian Statistical Internet Sites
  (NLA):
  www.nla.gov.au/oz/stats.html

## Universities, research institutes
Australian Defence Force
  Academy:
  www.defence.gov.au/adfa
Centre for Peace and Conflict
  Studies, University of Sydney:
  www.arts.usyd.edu.au/centres/
  cpacs
Centre for Strategic Studies,
  New Zealand:
  www.vuw.ac.nz/css

# Politics

## Archives

Archives (Electronic Australiana— NLA): www.nla.gov.au/ oz/#arch

Directory of Archives in Australia: www.archivists.org.au/directory/ asa_dir.htm

Register of Australian Archives and Manuscripts: www.nla.gov.au/raam

## Businesses

Australian Competition and Consumer Commission: www.accc.gov.au

Australian Stock Exchange (ASX): www.asx.com.au/asx

## Community, culture, events

Australian Local Government Association: www.alga.asn.au

## Databases, directories, search engines

Facts and figures relevant to NSW parliament and politics: www.parliament.nsw.gov.au/ Prod/Web/common.nsf/key/ resourcesfacts

Google Directory—Politics: http://directory.google.com/Top/ Regional/Oceania/Australia/ Society_and_Culture/Politics

Hurisearch—Human Rights Information and Documentation Systems, International— Huridocs: www.hurisearch.org

## Friends and foes

Australian universities (Australian Vice-Chancellors' Committee): www.avcc.edu.au

Online Opinion: www.onlineopinion.com.au

## Government agencies

Australian Commonwealth Government: www.australia.gov.au

New Zealand Government: www.govt.nz

## Indexes and databases

*Australian Public Affairs—Full Text* (APA-FT), RMIT Publishing, Melbourne, 1995–

*MicroMAIS (Multicultural Australia and Immigration Studies)*, Office of Multicultural Affairs and the Bureau of Immigration Studies, Canberra, 1992–

PAIS International, SilverPlatter, Boston MA, 1972–

## Legal

Austlii: www.austlii.edu.au

## Libraries

Australian Libraries Gateway — Library type—'Parliamentary': www.nla.gov.au/apps/libraries

Australian Government Information (NLA): www.nla.gov.au/oz/gov

Parliament of Australia Parliamentary Library: www.aph.gov.au/library

## News reports

ABC News: www.abc.net.au

Australian News Network: www.news.com.au

Australian newspapers online: www.nla.gov.au/npapers

CNN Interactive: www.cnn.com

Newsroom: www.newsroom.co.nz

Politics—ABC News Online: www.abc.net.au/news/politics

## Online communities

Ozlists: www.gu.edu.au/ozlists

## Organisations

Australian Democrats:
www.democrats.org.au
Australian Greens:
www.greens.org.au
Australian Labor Party:
www.alp.org.au
*Green Left Weekly*'s Progressive
Links: www.greenleft.org.
au/others.htm
Liberal Party of Australia:
www.liberal.org.au
National Party of Australia:
www.npa.org.au

## Periodicals

*The Bulletin*:
http://bulletin.ninemsn.com.au
*Green Left Weekly*:
www.greenleft.org.au

## Politicians, parliament

Parliament of Australia—*Hansard*:
www.aph.gov.au/hansard/index.
htm
Parliament of Australia—
Who's Who: www.aph.gov.au/
whoswho/index.htm

## Press releases

Press Releases Database,
Parliament of New South Wales:
www.parliament.nsw.gov.au/
Prod/Web/common.nsf/key/
resourcesMR
Prime Minister of New Zealand—
speeches and releases:
www.primeminister.govt.nz

## Reference

*Directory of Australian Associations*,
Information Australia,
Melbourne, 1978–
Moon, J. and Sharman, C.,
eds., 2003, *Australian Politics
and Government: The
Commonwealth, the States and
the Territories*, Cambridge
University Press, Cambridge UK

## Statistics

Australian Bureau of Statistics
Time Series: www.abs.gov.au
Australian Statistical Internet
Sites (NLA):
www.nla.gov.au/oz/stats.html

## Universities, research institutes

Department of Political Studies,
University of Auckland:
www.arts.auckland.ac.nz/pol

# Religion, spirituality

## Archives

Archive of Australian Judaica:
http://judaica.library.usyd.
edu.au
Archives (Electronic Australiana—
NLA): www.nla.gov.au/oz/#arch
Benedictine Community of New
Norcia Archive:
www.newnorcia.wa.edu.au/
archives.htm
Directory of Archives in Australia:
www.archivists.org.au/directory/
asa_dir.htm
Register of Australian Archives and
Manuscripts:
www.nla.gov.au/raam

## Businesses

Kompass Australia, Kompass New
Zealand: www.kompass.com

## Community, culture, events

Anglican Church of Australia
Diary: www.anglican.org.au
The Catholic Church of Australia:
www.catholic.org.au
Islamic Council of New South
Wales: www.icnsw.org.au

## Databases, directories, search engines

Australian Religion and Beliefs on the Internet:
www.nla.gov.au/oz/religion.html
beliefnet.com: www.beliefnet.com
The Scout Report: www.scout.cs.wisc.edu/scout/report

## Friends and foes

Australian universities (Australian Vice-Chancellors' Committee):
www.avcc.edu.au
Online Opinion:
www.onlineopinion.com.au

## Government agencies

Australian government entry point:
www.gov.au

## Indexes and databases

*Australasian Religion Index (ARI)*, Australian and New Zealand Theological Library Association and Centre for Information Studies, Charles Sturt University, Wagga Wagga, c. 1989–
*Australian Public Affairs—Full Text* (APA-FT), RMIT Publishing, Melbourne, 1995–

## Legal

Austlii: www.austlii.edu.au

## Libraries

Australian Libraries Gateway—Library type—'Religious':
www.nla.gov.au/apps/libraries

## News reports

*Australian Wesleyan*:
www.australian.wesleyan.org.au
*The Catholic Weekly*:
www.catholicweekly.com.au

## Online communities

Ozlists—Religion:
www.gu.edu.au/ozlists

## Organisations

Australian and New Zealand Society for Theological Studies:
wwwsoc.murdoch.edu.au/anzsts/home.html
Australian Association for the Study of Religions:
www.aasr.org.au
Executive Council of Australian Jewry: www.ecaj.org.au
Uniting Church in Australia:
http://uca.org.au

## Periodicals

Australian Religion Studies Review:
www.aasr.org.au/aasr/arsr.htm
*Journal for the Scientific Study of Religion*, Society for the Scientific Study of Religion, Storrs CN, 1961–

## Politicians, parliament

Parliament of Australia—Who's Who: www.aph.gov.au/whoswho/index.htm

## Press releases

Islamic Council of NSW press releases: www.icnsw.org.au
Press Release Centre:
www.pressrelease.com.au
Vatican Information Service:
www.vatican.va
World Council of Churches Press Corner: www.wcc-coe.org/wcc/press_corner/index-e.html

## Reference

Bible Gateway:
www.biblegateway.com
Bowker, J., ed., 1997, *The Oxford Dictionary of World Religions*, Oxford University Press, Oxford, New York
*Directory of Australian Associations*, Information Australia, Melbourne, 1978–

Martin, R.C., ed. c. 2004,
*Encyclopaedia of Islam and the
Muslim World*, Macmillan
Reference USA, Thomson/Gale,
New York

Schultz, J.D., West, J.G. Jr., and
MacLean, I. (eds), *Encyclopedia
of Religion in American Politics*,
Oryx Press, Phoenix AZ, 1999

**Statistics**

Australian Statistical Internet Sites
(NLA): www.nla.gov.au/oz/
stats.html

**Universities, research
institutes**

Department of Religious Studies,
University of Sydney: www.arts.
usyd.edu/departs/religion/

The School of History, Philosophy,
Religion, and Classics,
University of Queensland:
www.uq.edu.au/hprc

# Science

**Archives**

Archives (Electronic Australiana—
NLA): www.nla.gov.au/oz/#arch

Directory of Archives in Australia:
www.archivists.org.au/directory/
asa_dir.htm

Register of Australian Archives and
Manuscripts:
www.nla.gov.au/raam

**Businesses**

Ministry of Economic
Development, Companies Office
(NZ): www.companies.govt.nz

**Community, culture, events**

Food Science Australia
conferences:
www.foodscience.afisc.csiro.au

**Databases, directories,
search engines**

Chemical Industry Search Engine:
www.chemindustry.com

Chemweb: www.chemweb.com

Scirus: www.scirus.com

New Zealand Science and
Technology (Te Puna Web
Directory): http://webdirectory.
natlib.govt.nz/dir/en/nz/science-
and-technology

**Friends and foes**

Australian Science and Technology
Online Contact Directory:
www.asto.com.au/directory.php

Bright Sparcs:
www.asap.unimelb.edu.au/
bsparcs/bsparcshome.htm

Community of Science:
www.cos.com

**Government agencies**

Australian government entry point:
www.gov.au

**Indexes and databases**

*Applied Science & Technology
Index*, H.W. Wilson Co., New
York, 1958–

*Aquatic Sciences & Fisheries
Abstracts*, Cambridge Scientific
Abstracts, Bethesda MD, 1982–

*General Science Plus Text*, H.W.
Wilson, New York, 1994–

*Web of Science*, ISI, Philadelphia
PA, 1970–

**Legal**

Austlii: www.austlii.edu.au

**Libraries**

Australian Libraries Gateway —
Library type—'Science/
Technology': www.nla.gov.
au/apps/libraries

Food Science Australia Information Services: www.foodscience.afisc.csiro.au

## News reports
Google News Australia Sci/Tech: http://news.google.com.au
*Nova: Science in the News*: www.science.org.au/nova
Science News Online: www.sciencenews.org
ScienceDaily: www.sciencedaily.com

## Online communities
Ozlists—Science: www.gu.edu.au/ozlists

## Organisations
The Association of Consulting Engineers New Zealand Inc: www.acenz.org.nz
Australian Academy of Science: www.science.org.au

## Periodicals
*Nature*: www.nature.com
*New Scientist*: www.newscientist.com

## Politicians, parliament
Parliament of Australia—Who's Who: www.aph.gov.au/whoswho/index.htm

## Press releases
CSIRO Media Releases: www.csiro.au
EurekAlert! Science News: www.eurekalert.org/index.php
Press Release Centre: www.pressrelease.com.au

## Reference
Academic Press Dictionary of Science and Technology: www.harcourt.com/index.html

*Directory of Australian Associations*, Information Australia, Melbourne, 1978–
*McGraw-Hill Encyclopedia of Science & Technology*, 9th ed., McGraw-Hill Book Co., New York, c. 2002

## Statistics
Australian Statistical Internet Sites (NLA): www.nla.gov.au/oz/stats.html

## Universities, research institutes
Faculty of Science, University of New South Wales: www.science.unsw.edu.au

# Sports
## Archives
Archives (Electronic Australiana — NLA): www.nla.gov.au/oz/#arch
Directory of Archives in Australia: www.archivists.org.au/directory/asa_dir.htm
Register of Australian Archives and Manuscripts: www.nla.gov.au/raam

## Businesses
Australian Sports Industry Directory: www.aussport.com.au
Golf.com: www.golf.com

## Community, culture, events
Australian Sports Commission Conferences and Events: www.ausport.gov.au
Beijing Organising Committee for the Games of the 29th Olympiad: http://en.beijing-2008.org

## Databases, directories, search engines
SOCIC: Sociology of Sport: www.sosig.ac.uk/roads/subject-listing/World-cat/socsport.html

Sport Information Resource Centre:
www.sirc.ca

**Friends and foes**
Australian Sports Science
Directory:
www.ais.org.au/lsas/ssd.asp

**Government agencies**
Australian Institute of Health and
Welfare: www.aihw.gov.au
Australian Sports Commission:
www.ausport.gov.au
Sport and Recreation (ACT):
www.sport.act.gov.au
West Australian Institute of Sport:
www.wais.org.au

**Indexes and databases**
*Sport Discus*, Silver Platter, Boston
MA, 1975–
*Web of Science*, ISI, Philadelphia
PA, 1970–

**Legal**
Austlii: www.austlii.edu.au

**Libraries**
Australian Libraries Gateway:
www.nla.gov.au/apps/libraries

**News reports**
ABC Sport Online:
www.abc.net.au/sport
The Age Sport:
www.sportstoday.com.au
Wide World of Sports:
www.wideworldofsports.ninemsn.
com.au/homepage.asp

**Online communities**
Ozlists—Sport:
www.gu.edu.au/ozlists

**Organisations**
Australian Council for Health,
Physical Education and
Recreation: www.achper.org.au

Australian Rugby Union:
www.rugby.com.au
Australian Swimming:
www.ausswim.telstra.com.au
British Society of Sport History:
www2.umist.ac.uk/sport/SPORTS
%20HISTORY/index2.html
International Australian Football
Council: www.iafc.org.au
Official Website of the Olympic
Movement: www.olympic.org
Sport & Recreation New Zealand:
www.sparc.org.nz
National Rugby League:
www.nrl.com.au
The Official Australian Football
League website: www.
afl.com.au/home/default.htm
Soccer NSW:
www.soccernsw.com.au
Sport Central:
www.sportcentral.com.au
Sport SA: www.sportsa.org.au
Surfing Australia:
www.surfingaustralia.com.au

**Periodicals**
Sports Medicine Australia: www.
sma.org.au/publications/JSMS

**Politicians, parliament**
Parliament of Australia—Who's
Who: www.aph.gov.au/
whoswho/index.htm

**Press releases**
Press Release Centre:
www.pressrelease.com.au

**Reference**
*Berkshire Encyclopedia of World
Sport*, Berkshire Publishing,
Great Barrington MA, 2005

**Statistics**
Cricinfo: http://aus.cricinfo.com/

## Universities, research institutes

Center for the Study of Sport in Society, Northeastern University, Boston MA:
www.sportinsociety.org

Centre for Healthy Activities, Sport and Exercise, University of the Sunshine Coast:
www.usc.edu.au/Research/Centres/CHASE

Sportscience: http://sportsci.org

# Tourism, travel

## Archives

Archives (Electronic Australiana—NLA): www.nla.gov.au/oz/#arch

Directory of Archives in Australia:
www.archivists.org.au/directory/asa_dir.htm

Register of Australian Archives and Manuscripts:
www.nla.gov.au/raam

## Businesses

Excite Travel:
www.excite.com/travel

Fodor's: www.fodors.com

Lonely Planet:
www.lonelyplanet.com.au

## Community, culture, events

Department of Industry, Tourism and Resources (Australia) Tourism Industry Events:
www.industry.gov.au

## Databases, directories, search engines

Altis: The guide to internet resources in hospitality, leisure, sport and tourism:
www.altis.ac.uk/

Maporama: http://maporama.com

RACQ Travel Planner:
www.racq.com.au

Travel Australia:
www.travelaustralia.com.au

## Friends and foes

Tourism New Zealand:
www.tourisminfo.govt.nz

## Government agencies

Department of Industry, Tourism and Resources (Australia):
www.industry.gov.au

Tourism Research Australia:
www.btr.gov.au

## Indexes and databases

*ABI/Inform Global*, UMI, Ann Arbor MI, 1971–

*Australian Tourism Index*, RMIT Publishing, Melbourne, 1982–

## Legal

Austlii: www.austlii.edu.au

## Libraries

Australian Libraries Gateway:
www.nla.gov.au/apps/libraries

## News reports

Tourism Queensland News:
www.tq.com.au

## Online communities

Ozlists: www.gu.edu.au/ozlists

## Organisations

International Air Transport Association (IATA):
www.iata.org/index.htm

New Zealand Gay and Lesbian Tourism Association (NZGLTA):
www.gaytravel.net.nz/nz/nzglta.html

World Tourism Organization (WTO): www.world-tourism.org

## Periodicals

*Annals of Tourism Research*,
  Pergamon, New York, 1973–
*Fine Travel Magazine*:
  www.finetravel.com

## Politicians, parliament

Parliament of Australia—
  Who's Who: www.aph.gov.
  au/whoswho/index.htm

## Press releases

Press Release Centre:
  www.pressrelease.com.au
Tourism Queensland press
  releases: www.tq.com.au

## Reference

Medlik, S. 2003, *Dictionary of
  Travel, Tourism and Hospitality*,
  3rd edn, Butterworth-
  Heinemann, Oxford
Perry-Castañeda Library Map
  Collection: www.lib.utexas.
  edu/Libs/PCL/Map_collection/
  Map_collection.html
Youell, R. 2003, *Complete A–Z
  Leisure, Travel and Tourism
  Handbook*, Hodder &
  Stoughton, London

## Statistics

Australian Bureau of Statistics:
  www.abs.gov.au
Australian Statistical Internet
  Sites (NLA):
  www.nla.gov.au/oz/stats.html
*Compendium of Tourism Statistics*
  2004, World Tourism Organization Publications, Madrid
Tourism—Statistics New Zealand:
  www.stats.govt.nz/economy/
  industry/tourism.htm

## Universities, research institutes

Sustainable Tourism, University
  of the Sunshine Coast:
  www.usc.edu.au/Research/
  Institutes/iSHaRE/
  ProgramsStrengths/ST.htm
WeatherNet: http://
  cirrus.sprl.umich.edu/wxnet

# BIBLIOGRAPHY

ABC Legal Department 1997, 'Reporting the courts', in *The ABC All-Media Law Handbook for Journalists, Presenters, Programmers, Authors, Editors and Publishers*, ABC Enterprises, Sydney

Ackermann, E. and Hartman, K. 2003, *Searching and Researching on the Internet and the World Wide Web*, 3rd edn, Franklin Beedle, Wilsonville OR

Alexander, J. and Tate, M.A. 1999, 'Evaluating web resources', Widener University's Wolfgram Memorial Library, www2.widener.edu/Wolfgram-Memorial-Library/webevaluation/ webeval.htm

Alexander, J. and Tate, M.A. 1999, *Web Wisdom: How to Evaluate and Create Information Quality on the Web*, Lawrence Erlbaum Associates, Mahwah NJ

Alysen B., Sedorkin G., Oakham M. and Patching R. 2003, *Reporting in a Multimedia World*, Allen & Unwin, Sydney

Archer, H. 2000, *Untangling the Web: An Australian Research Guide to Internet Sites*, New Holland Publishers, Sydney

Australian Bureau of Statistics 1989–, *Catalogue of Publications and Products*, ABS, Canberra

Bass, F. 2001, *The Associated Press Guide to Internet Research and Reporting*, Perseus Publishing, Cambridge MA

Begg, P. 2004, 'Channel project slammed', *The Geelong Advertiser*, 19 May

Berkman, R. I. 2000, *Find it Fast: How to Uncover Expert Information on Any Subject*, 5th edn, HarperResource, New York

Best, J. c. 2001, *Damned Lies and Statistics: Untangling Numbers from the Media, Politicians, and Activists*, University of California Press, Berkeley

Bingham E. and Andrews, J. 2003, 'Fire-trucks cover for ambulance', *The New Zealand Herald*, 1 November

Blum, D. 2002, 'Investigating science', *Nieman Reports*, Cambridge, Fall

Booth, W.C., Colomb, G.C. and Williams, J.M. c. 2003, *The Craft of Research*, University of Chicago Press, Chicago

Bromley, M. 2002, 'Journalism Still Dodges the Big Questions: A View from Australia', *Zoned for Debate*, Department of Journalism, New York University, http://journalism.nyu.edu/pubzone/debate/ forum.1.essay.bromley.html

Brown, M. 2003, Email interview, 15 January

Burkle-Young F.A. and Maley, S.R. 1997, *The Research Guide for the Digital Age: A New Handbook to Research and Writing for the Serious Student*, University Press of America, Lanham MD

Burton, B. 2004, Email interview, 29 March

Callahan, C. 1999, *A Journalist's Guide to the Internet: The Net as a Reporting Tool*, Allyn and Bacon, Boston MA

Cannon, C.M. 2001, 'The Real Computer Virus', *American Journalism Review*, April, AMJNewsLink, http://amj.newslink.org/ ajrcarlapr01.html

Castle, P. 2003, Interview, Queensland University of Technology, 1 August

Cater, A. 2004, Email, 10 March

Chulov, M. 2002, *The Australian*, Media, 22–28 August

Clark, P. 2003, Email interview, 16 January

Colley A. 2000, ' The BBC's Leading Investigative Broadcast Researcher', in Hane, P.J., c. 2000. *Super Searchers in the News: The Online Secrets of Journalists and News Researchers*, ed. Reva Basch, Information Today, Medford NJ

Cohn, V. 2003. Lewis Cope 2001, *News and Numbers: A Guide to Reporting Statistical Claims and Controversies in Health and Other Fields*, 2nd edn, State University Press, Ames IA

Correy, Stan. 2004, Interview, Sydney, 20 May

Dale, D. 2004, Telephone interview, 2 February

Dayton, L. 2003. 'Flu fighters see the light after a beer', *The Australian*, 3 June

Department of the Parliamentary Library 2003, 'Crime and Candidacy', Parliamentary Library Current Issues Brief, no. 22, 2002–03, www.aph.gov.au/library/pubs/cib/2002-03/03cib22.pdf

De Wolk, R. 2001, *Introduction to Online Journalism: Publishing News and Information*, Allyn and Bacon, Boston MA

Dickie, P. 1988, *The Road to Fitzgerald: Revelations of Corruption Spanning Four Decades* University of Queensland Press, Brisbane

Dickie, P. 2002, 'Getting past spin cycle—part one', The Brisbane Institute, 11 July, www.brisinst.org.au/resources/dickie_phil_spin1.html

Dodson, L. 2000, 'Company donations heavily favour Libs', *Australian Financial Review*, 22 June

Dullroy, J. 2003, 'School of thought to enter the classroom', *The Courier-Mail*, 26 June

Edmistone, L. 2003, 'Parents angry over hospitals' scan refusal', *The Courier-Mail*, 26 June

Ellicott, J. 2003, 'Parliamentary books sail', *The Australian*, 14 February

'Evaluating the quality of information on the internet', The Virtual Chase, www.virtualchase.com/quality

Feola, C.J. and Leslie, J. 1994, 'The Nexis nightmare', *American Journalism Review*, July/August, p. 38

Field, M. 2000, *Writer's Guide to Research: An Invaluable Guide to Gathering Materials for Features, Novels and Non-Fiction Books*, 2nd edn, How To Books, Oxford UK

Fiske, P. 2004, Interview, 3 February

Fist, S. 2000, 'Watchdogs we need to watch', *The Australian*, 15 August

*Freedom of Information Review: An Australian Journal*, University of Tasmania, www.foi.law.utas.edu.au/foi_rev.html

Gach, G.1997, *Writers.net: Every Writer's Essential Guide to Online Resources and Opportunities*, Prima Publishing, Rocklin, CA

Garrison, B. 1998, *Computer-assisted Reporting*, 2nd edn, Erlbaum Associates, Mahwah NJ

Garrison, B. 2004, *Online News and the Public*, ed. M.B. Salwen, B. Garrison and P.D. Driscoll, Erlbaum Associates, Mahwah NJ

Germov, J. and Williams, L. 1999, *Get Great Information Fast*, Allen & Unwin, Sydney

Gittins, R. 2000, 'Too many e-tail holes in the net', *Sydney Morning Herald*, 1 March

Gold, B. 2001, *InfoWar in Cyberspace: Researcher on the Net*, Booklocker.com

Goot, M. 2002, 'Reporting the Polls' in S. Tanner (ed.) *Journalism: Investigation & Research*, Longman, Sydney

Grabowicz, P. 2002a, 'Researching people on the internet I', *Online Journalism Review*, www.ojr.org/ojr/technology/1027538596.php

Grabowicz, P. 2002b, 'Researching people on the internet II', *Online Journalism Review*, www.ojr.org/ojr/technology/1028068074.php

Greber, J. 2000, 'Complaints against police pile up', *Courier-Mail*, 11 November

Hager, N. and Burton, B. 1999, *Secrets and Lies: The Anatomy of an Anti-environmental PR Campaign*, Craig Potton Publishing, Nelson, New Zealand

Hall, J. 2001, *Online journalism: A Critical Primer*, Pluto Press, Sydney

Hane, P.J. c. 2000, *Super Searchers in the News: The Online Secrets of Journalists and News Researchers*, Information Today, Medford NJ

Harrison, K. and Cossins, A. 1993, *Documents, Dossiers and the Inside Dope: How to Use the Commonwealth Freedom of Information Act*, 2nd edn, Allen & Unwin, Sydney

Hawkins, S. 1996, 'Director and playwright trade blows over claims of heresy', *Daily Telegraph*, 2 April

Hedley, T. 2003, 'Flood cover-up', *Courier-Mail*, 24 June

Henninger, M. 2003, *The Hidden Web: Finding Quality Information on the Net*, University of New South Wales Press, Sydney

Hetherington, S. 2000, Lecture, Queensland University of Technology, 28 March

Hoffman, A. 1999, *Research for Writers*, 7th edn, A & C Black, London

Houston, B. 2004, *Computer-Assisted Reporting: A Practical Guide*, 3rd edn, Bedford/St Martins Press, Boston MA

Houston, B., Bruzzese, L. and Weinberg, S. 2002, *The Investigative Reporter's Handbook*, 4th edn, St Martin's Press, New York

Hutchinson, S. 2003, 'Under-age, overproof', *The Australian*, 22 July

Israel, J. and Vaughan, A. 2000, 'Nursing Homes rated unacceptable', *Sydney Morning Herald*, 2 March

Internet Detective, www.sosig.ac.uk/desire/internet-detective.html

Itule, B.D. and Anderson, D.A. 1999, *News Writing and Reporting for Today's Media*, McGraw-Hill, New York

Jackman, C. 2003a, 'Private school enrolments boom', *The Australian*, 27 February

Jackman, C. 2003b, 'Savings in weaning mums off welfare', *The Australian*, 11 June

Johnson, R.S. and Knox, D.J. 2001, *Find Anyone Fast: Easy-to-use Guide to Finding Anyone Anywhere*, 3rd edn, Independent Publishing Group, Chicago ILL

Kennedy, A.J. 2002, *The Rough Guide to the Internet: 2003 edition*, Rough Guides, London

Kerin, J. 2001, 'US ignites corporate health fear', *The Australian*, 2 April

King, D. 2003, 'Misunderstood maggots help to fight crime', *The Australian*, 11 June

Kirk, E.E. 2001, 'Information and its counterfeits: Propaganda, misinformation and disinformation', www.library.jhu.edu/researchhelp/general/evaluating/counterfeit.html

Krantz, M. 1996, *Ideas and Research*, Writer's Digest Books, Cincinnati OH

Kroger, Brooke n.d. 'Journalism with a Scholar's Intent', in *Zoned for Debate*, Department of Journalism, New York University, www.nyu.edu/gsas/dept/journal/forum.1.essay.kroger.html

Levitt, Steven n.d. 'Sample selection in the estimation of air bag and seatbelt effectiveness', http://ideas.repec.org/p/nbr/nberwo/ 7210.html

Lim, A. 2003, Telephone interview, 2 February

Lockwood, T. and Scott, K. 1999, *A Writer's Guide to the Internet*, Allison & Busby, London

Lorenz, A.L. and Vivian, J. 1996, *News: Reporting and Writing*, Allyn & Bacon, Boston MA

Martin, L., O'Loughlin, T. and AAP 1999, 'Liberals fail to repay $4.5m "shonky" loan', *Sydney Morning Herald*, 2 February

McGregor, J. and Sedorkin, G. 2002, *Interviewing*, Allen & Unwin, Sydney

McGuire, M. et al. c. 2002, *The Internet Handbook for Writers, Researchers and Journalists*, Guilford Press, New York

McHugh, S. 1993, *Minefields and Miniskirts—Australian Women and the Vietnam War*, Doubleday (Lothian, 2005)

McHugh, S. 1989, *The Snowy—The People Behind the Power*, Heinemann (Harper Collins 1995)

McHugh, S. 1996, *Cottoning On—Stories of Australian Cottongrowing*, Hale & Iremonger

McKinnon, M. 2000, '$630m splurged on consultants', *Courier-Mail*, 24 July

McKnight, D. 1999, Lecture notes, University of Technology, Sydney

Martin, L., O'Loughlin, T. and AAP, 1999, 'Liberals fail to repay $4.5m "shonky" loan', *Sydney Morning Herald*, 2 February

Meryment, E., 2002, Lecture, Queensland University of Technology, Brisbane, 20 August

Metter, E. 1999, *Facts in a Flash: A Research Guide for Writers*, Writer's Digest Books, Cincinnati OH

Meyer, P. 2002, *Precision Journalism: A Reporter's Introduction to Social Science Methods*, 4th edn, Rowman & Littlefield, New York

Miller, L. C. 1998, *Power Journalism: Computer-Assisted Reporting*, Harcourt Brace College Publishers, Fort Worth TX

Mintz, A. (ed.) 2002, *Web of Deception: Misinformation on the Internet*, Information Today, Medford NJ

Mitchell, S. 2000, 'Source of angst', *The Australian*, 12 September

Murphy, D. 2000, 'High roller named as "sex trader"', *Sydney Morning Herald*, 27 May

Northmore, D. 1996, *Lifting the Lid: A Guide to Investigative Research*, Cassell, London, New York

O'Loughlin, T. 2002, 'Law goes soft on financial hard sell', *Sydney Morning Herald*, 19 June

Paul, N. 1999a, *Computer Assisted Research: A Guide to Tapping Online Information*, 4th edn, Bonus Books, Chicago

Paul, N. (ed.) 1999b, *When Nerds and Words Collide: Reflections on the Development of Computer-Assisted Reporting*, Poynter, Florida

Paul, N. and Williams, M. 1999, *Great Scouts! CyberGuides for Subject Searching on the Web*, CyberAge Books Inc., Medford NJ

Paul, N., Keirstad, B. and Shedden, D. 1996, 'The Answer's Here—What's your Question?', posted to FACSNET 23 April / revised 2 February 2000, www.facsnet.org/tools/ref_tutor/compresearch/ answers.php3

Pearson, M. 2002, The new 'multi-journalism': Journalists' and educators' perceptions of the influences of the internet upon journalism and its implications for journalism education, PhD thesis, Bond University, www.bond.edu.au/hss/staff/ mpearson-phd.htm

Pearson, M. 2004, *The Journalists Guide to Media Law*, 2nd edn, Allen & Unwin, Sydney

Pfaffenberger, B. 1996, *Web Search Strategies*, MIS Press, New York

Piper, P.S. 2000, 'Better read that again: Web hoaxes and misinformation', *Searcher*, vol. 8, no. 8, Western Washington University, www.infotoday.com/searcher/sep00/piper.htm

Quinn, S. 2001, *Newsgathering on the Net*, 2nd edn, Macmillan, Melbourne

Ramsay, A. 1999, 'Timor: A debt dishonoured', *Sydney Morning Herald*, 25 September

Reddick, R. and King, E. 2000, *The Online Journalist: Using the Internet and other Electronic Resources*, 3rd edn, Harcourt Brace College, Fort Worth TX

*Report to the Honourable Premier of Queensland and the Queensland Cabinet of an Investigation into Allegations by Mr Kevin Lindeberg and Allegations by Mr Gordon Harris and Mr John Reynolds*, Mr Anthony Morris QC and Mr Edward Howard, 1996.

Ricketson, M. and Snell, R. 2002, 'FOI: Threatened by governments, underused by journalists—still a sharp tool', in S. Tanner (ed.) *Journalism: Investigation and Research*, Longman, Sydney

Roszak, T. c. 1994, *The Cult of Information: A Neo-Luddite Treatise on High Tech, Artificial Intelligence, and the True Art of Thinking*, University of California Press, Berkeley CA

Robotham, J. 2002, 'Surgery recovery easier for quitters', *Sydney Morning Herald* Weekend Edition, 12–13 January

Seib, P.M. 2000, *Going Live: Getting the News Right in a Real-Time, Online World*. Rowman & Littlefield, Lanham MD

Schlein, A. 2002, *Find It Online: The Complete Guide to Online Research*, 3rd edn, Facts on Demand Press, Tempe AZ

Sherman, C. and Price, G.C. 2001, *The Invisible Web: Uncovering Information Sources Search Engines Can't See*, Cyberage Books, Medford NJ

Silva, J.L. 2003, 'When a museum falls victim to war', *Philippine Daily Inquirer*, 23 April

Smith, W. 2000, 'A sick and sorry society', *Courier-Mail*, 17 March

Spark, D. 1999, *Investigative Reporting: A Study in Technique*, Focal Press, Oxford, Boston

Starr, D. 2002, 'Teaching journalism students to report on science', *Nieman Reports*, Fall, Cambridge

Stauber, J. and Rampton, S. c. 1995, *Toxic Sludge is Good For You*, Common Courage Press, Monroe ME

Steketee, M. 2003, 'Still work in progress', *The Weekend Australian*, 7–8 June

Stewart, C. 1996, 'Revealed: Secret offer for troops to Vietnam', *The Australian*, 1 January

Stewart, C. 2001, 'For all the fish in the sea', *The Weekend Australian Magazine*, 8–9 December

Stewart, C. 2002, 'Navy missed doomed boat', *The Weekend Australian*, 29–30 June

Tanner, S. (ed.) 2002, *Journalism: Investigation and Research*, Longman, Sydney

Thomas, H. 2003, Interview, 15 December

Tingle, L. 2000, 'A conspiracy of dunces', *Sydney Morning Herald*, 20 May

Wainwright, R. 2003, 'A new rule book for our politicians? We'd like to see that', *Sydney Morning Herald*, 3 February

Ward, M. 2002, *Journalism Online*, Focal Press, Oxford

Waterford, J. 1999a, 'The Changing Role of a Newspaper Editor', *Australian Studies in Journalism*, no. 8, pp. 3–17

Waterford, J. 1999b, 'Journalists, freedom of information legislation and investigative reporting', address to University of Queensland students, Brisbane, 7 October

Waterford, J. 2002, 'The editor's position', in S. Tanner (ed.), *Journalism: Investigation and Research*, Longman, Sydney

Weaver, B. 2002, 'The computer as an essential tool', in S. Tanner (ed.), *Journalism: Investigation and Research*, Longman, Sydney

Weaver, B. 2003, *Catch the Wave: How to Find Good Information on the Internet Fast*, Informit, RMIT University Press, Melbourne

Weinberg, S. 1996, *The Reporter's Handbook: An Investigator's Guide to Documents and Techniques*, 3rd edn, St Martins Press, New York

Wickham, K. 2002, *Math Tools for Journalists*, 2nd edn., Marion Street Press, Oak Park IL

Wilkinson, J. 2002, *MPs' Entitlements, Occasional Paper No. 8*, New South Wales Parliamentary Library Research Service, Sydney

Willey, S. 2000, 'The pitfalls of cyberspace and electronic database research: Who sells what to whom for which audience?' *Journalism & Mass Communication Educator*, Summer